# YOUR Unforgettable

# life

only you can choose the legacy

you leave

Jennifer Schuchmann
and Craig Chapin

Beacon Hill Press of Kansas City
Kansas City, Missouri

ISBN 083-412-1875

Printed in the
United States of America
Cover Design: Doug Bennett

### Library of Congress Cataloging-in-Publication Data

Chapin, Craig, 1965-
Your unforgettable life : only you can choose the legacy you leave / Craig Chapin, Jennifer Schuchmann.
    p. cm.
Includes bibliographical references.
ISBN 0-8341-2187-5 (pbk.)
1. Parenting—Religious aspects—Christianity. I. Schuchmann, Jennifer, 1966- II. Title.

BV4529.C43 2005
248.8'45—dc22

2005012338

10   9   8   7   6   5   4   3   2   1

The authors dedicate this book to their families—
to the thousandth generation.

# Contents

# Acknowledgments

If a legacy is the sum of seemingly insignificant choices, then writing a book is a lesson in how to leave a legacy. Many people influenced this book in what seemed like insignificant ways at the time, but the book is better because of their contributions. It is impossible to acknowledge them all.

Thank you, everyone who allowed us to share your story. We learned from you.

Thank you to those who read and commented on early drafts of the manuscript. You know who you are, but you'll never know how much you helped.

Thank you, Chip MacGregor, for your dedication to this project. May God bless your new endeavor.

Thank you, Judi Perry and Bonnie Perry, at Beacon Hill. You both believed in this book from the beginning. We appreciate you and the entire Beacon Hill staff.

From Craig:

I thank my wonderful wife, kids, and parents, whose love and support continue to shape who I am and who I can become. Godspeed.

From Jennifer:

Teisha Moseley—When we met, I thought I would teach you what it meant to be a writer. Instead, you've taught me what it means to be a friend.

Cecil Murphey—You were there for the idea that birthed this book, you stayed with me during all the labor pains of writing it, and you were one of the first to hold it in your capable, mentoring hands. Thank you for taking such care of both baby and mom. Your friendship is like your writing—intimate, caring, and warm.

David and Jordan—I love you both. Thank you.

Most of all we would like to thank Jesus Christ, who left the ultimate example of a legacy and whose love and grace extend forever.

# part 1

## A Legacy: Do You Have One?

*The only thing you take with you when*
*you're gone is what you leave behind.*
—John Allston

*What is popularly called fame is nothing but*
*an empty name and a legacy from paganism.*
—Desiderius Erasmus (c. 1466–1536)

*He who has done his best for his own time*
*has lived for all times.*
—Johann von Schiller

*By faith Abel offered God a better sacrifice than Cain did.*
*By faith he was commended as a righteous man,*
*when God spoke well of his offerings.*
*And by faith he still speaks, even though he is dead.*
—Heb. 11:4

# 1

# You Have a LEGACY

*Oh, if a man tried to take his time on earth*
*and prove before he died*
*what one man's life could be worth,*
*I wonder what would happen to this world.*
                    —Engraved on singer Harry Chapin's tombstone

In his hometown of Huntington, New York, it wasn't his celebrity status that they liked—it was his hugs. They knew him as a neighbor, friend, and philanthropist. To his fans he was a master storyteller and folk singer. To music insiders, he was a mediocre talent. But to his family he was anything but mediocre; he meant everything to them.

Late singer, songwriter, and master storyteller Harry Chapin[1] raised millions of dollars for world hunger before his death in a car accident in 1981. His personal legacy was a rich one, both publicly and privately, but perhaps his greatest gift was to help others think about the legacies they might leave.

His 1974 chart-topping single, "Cat's in the Cradle," was about a father who passed his legacy on to his son only to realize too late that it wasn't the legacy he desired to leave. Chapin was known as a singer who could tell a powerful story. Though his voice is silent now, the words of this song still speak.

*A child arrived just the other day,*
*He came to the world in the usual way.*

*But there were planes to catch and bills to pay.*
*He learned to walk while I was away.*
*And he was talking 'fore I knew it, and as he grew,*
*He'd say, "I'm gonna be like you, Dad.*
*You know, I'm gonna be like you."*

*And the cat's in the cradle and the silver spoon,*
*Little Boy Blue and the man in the moon.*
*"When you comin' home, Dad?" "I don't know when,*
*But we'll get together then.*
*You know, we'll have a good time then."*

*My son turned ten just the other day.*
*He said, "Thanks for the ball, Dad. Come on—let's play.*
*Can you teach me to throw?" I said, "Not today.*
*I got a lot to do." He said, "That's OK."*
*And he walked away, but his smile never dimmed,*
*It said, "I'm gonna be like him, yeah.*
*You know, I'm gonna be like him."*

*Well, he came from college just the other day*
*So much like a man I just had to say,*
*"Son, I'm proud of you. Can you sit for a while?"*
*He shook his head, and he said with a smile,*
*"What I'd really like, Dad, is to borrow the car keys.*
*See you later. Can I have them, please?"*

*I've long since retired, and my son's moved away.*
*I called him up just the other day.*
*I said, "I'd like to see you if you don't mind."*
*He said, "I'd love to, Dad, if I could find the time.*
*You see, my new job's a hassle, and the kids with the flu,*
*But it's sure nice talkin' to you, Dad.*
*It's been sure nice talking to you."*

*As I hung up the phone, it occurred to me,*
*He'd grown up just like me.*
*My boy was just like me.*

These lyrics, penned by Chapin's wife, Sandy, are a poignant reminder that we all leave a legacy whether or not it's intentional. Ironically, the demand for Chapin's concerts and appearances grew with his success. He was en route to one of those concerts when he died on the Long Island Expressway. After his death, friends were quoted as saying how alone Chapin felt while traveling because he missed his family. The very song that helped to create his legacy ultimately made him so famous that it required him to travel more, taking him away from the family he loved.

## Everyone Has a Legacy

We all leave a legacy.

Some might disagree by saying, "I'm not dead yet," or "Only famous people have legacies." The truth is that we don't have to be rich, famous, or even dead to have a legacy. Just like the father in the song, we leave our legacy—our imprint—on the hearts and minds of those who know us best. The little decisions we make on a daily basis and the behaviors we repeat over time are the things that people remember long after we move, change jobs, or die. Our legacy is the sum of every choice we make. Finish the following sentences:

My mother always . . .

My father never . . .

My friend would . . .

The end of each sentence is part of the legacy that person has left with us. It's how we remember him or her. Some have inherited positive legacies:

"My mother always prayed."

"My father never missed a Sunday at church."

"My friend would give me the shirt off his back."

But then, sometimes the legacies we receive aren't the things we would choose:

"My mother always criticized me."

"My father never came to my games."

"My friend talked about me behind my back."

How would our children, friends, and coworkers finish the following sentences about us?

He always said . . .

She used to . . .

He never tried to . . .

The answers to these questions reveal the legacy we're leaving the people close to us. Even people like Oprah Winfrey or Bill Gates, who have a very public legacy, leave a private legacy to those who know them best. The dad in Chapin's song was obviously outstanding in his job, but the private legacy he left to his son at home wasn't so positive.

For another example, consider a career politician at his visitation and funeral. While his fellow government servants talk about the difference the deceased made in his job, his children rarely talk about such things. Instead, they remember the quiet moments, the laughter, and the personal, intimate details of their father. This reminds us that we each have two legacies, the public persona that often involves our jobs or church activities, and the private, personal legacy left to those closest to us. Perhaps the best definition of success is how our personal and public legacies match up.

We may never have the kind of public legacy of Bill Gates and Oprah, but we have family, friends, and coworkers who will continue to respond to the private legacy we leave long after we've changed jobs, moved, or died.

## An Inherited Legacy

Patrick Borders is the father of two children, a solid member of his metro-Atlanta area church, and a man who loves his country. He's probably a lot like someone you work with or know from church: strong, dependable, and unassuming. Patrick left the corporate world to become a full-time writer, and during the transition he spent time interviewing his grandmother Ivy for a book project. It was during one of these interviews that Patrick learned more about Ivy's father, Walter Collins, Patrick's great-grandfather.

Walter Collins loved the United States so much that he enlisted in the military in 1903. When Ivy was born, he was stationed at Bedloe's Island (now Liberty Island, the location of the Statue of Liberty). He named his daughter Ivy Liberty Collins after the statue that meant so much to him. Always an optimist, Walter believed that the United States offered opportunities not found anywhere else in the world. With those opportunities came individual responsibilities to make wise use of them, and he did his best to take advantage of them.

Walter loved people, and he studied them endlessly. He instilled in Ivy a desire to understand others and their motivations. He had a strong sense of right and wrong, so strong that he lived his life by a strict code of honor—he did the right thing no matter what.

As Patrick processed the information he gathered about his great-grandfather, he realized that Walter's legacy had passed down through his grandmother and was alive in him. Patrick made the transition from corporate career to freelance writer to take advantage of the opportunities and legacy given to him. Despite an initial lack of work, he remained optimistic, as did Walter. His desire to do what was right provided the motivation for several foreign mission trips to help underprivileged children.

What startled Patrick most when he discovered those parallels with Walter was that he had inherited his legacy from a man he had never met. Patrick's great-grandfather, Walter Collins, died 11 years before Patrick was born.

## A Legacy Lived Out

Legacies aren't always inherited; sometimes they're experienced. Born and raised in California, Scott was only three when his mother left home for good. Scott never understood why; he only felt the pain of her rejection. When Scott was four years old, his father remarried. Too young to articulate his emotional needs, Scott sensed that this woman would not fill them. His stepmother was insecure and dominating. She monopolized his dad into spending more time with her and less time with him. Scott compensated by spending more time with his dog.

When his stepmother moved in, so did John, her son. John also knew the pain of divorce, and unlike his mother, he saw what was happening to his little stepbrother. Determined to compensate for the losses in Scott's life, John bonded with Scott as only boys can do. Through play, he and Scott grew close via wrestling matches and knuckle sandwiches.

John was 10 years older, and he took his mentoring responsibilities seriously. He taught Scott to throw a baseball, pass a football, and kick a soccer ball. Later, he coached Scott's teams. Even after John left for college, he returned home to spend time with Scott, attending the games his father and stepmother never found time to attend. John's coaching taught Scott more than how to play sports. It taught him how to take risks, how to trust, and how to be a man.

One day while educating the boy on the finer points of throwing a curveball, John lost his patience. Scott was goofing around—more interested in doing impressions than learning the correct fingering. John picked up a ball and hurled it at the fence.

That night as Scott lay in bed, he worried that John might not come back. For the first time, Scott thought about the sacrifices his stepbrother made in giving up time with friends his own age to spend it with him. John often stayed up late finishing his college homework or studying for upcoming exams. He defended Scott to his father and stepmother, even when it meant taking sides against family. John made him feel as if he were the most important person in his life. Scott went to sleep not sure if his stepbrother would be there in the morning.

The next morning before he awoke, a soft thud hit his sheets. He opened his eyes to see a baseball lobbed gently onto his bed, and then another and another. He jumped up in time to miss the next one. By the time he had gotten his clothes on, his floor was covered with balls that had hit the bed and rolled off. Finally, he heard John's gentle words from the hallway: "I'm sorry for losing my temper yesterday. Can we try again?"

John's devotion changed Scott's life. He taught Scott passion for sports and life. Years later, Scott became a coach for both his daughter and son's soccer teams. Today he continues to pass on the values he learned from his stepbrother, both on and off the field. John has left a legacy that lives on in Scott and Scott's kids, who know that their dad will always be there, just as John was there for Scott.

## A Chosen Legacy

One meaning of "legacy" is a gift made by will, especially of money or other personal property. It can be something transmitted by or received from an ancestor, a predecessor, or the past.

"By will" is the interesting part of the definition. While the word refers to the legal document created by a lawyer, for our purposes it also has another meaning. We have a will, the part of us that makes choices and decisions. A legacy is a result of those choices, of doing what *we will*. It is deliberate, conscious, and volitional. There are consequences for the choices we make, and only we can decide what kind of legacy we *will* have.

Leaving a legacy isn't about a single choice or a one-time event in our life, good or bad. It isn't about how much money we donate to charity or having a building named after us. It isn't about the worst things we've done in the past or the best things we'll do in the future. Rather, it is the culmination of the seemingly insignificant things we do each day—the things that add up and are remembered later.

Most of us have probably never heard of John, the kind stepbrother, or Walter, the great-grandfather, but we probably know someone like them. Both of these men lived their lives deliberately. For Walter, the insignificant decisions he made on a daily basis added up to a lifestyle, passed on to his daughter, Ivy. She created her own legacy when she passed those values, morals, and choices on to her grandson as she helped raise him. And John made a choice to commit himself to his little brother regardless of the personal sacrifices it cost him.

Patrick and Scott both received legacies from their families; so did the son in Chapin's song. His father passed on a legacy of choosing work over family. His son learned that lesson so well that even years later, he "couldn't" visit his father because, like his father, he had other priorities.

We make decisions about what our legacy will be, whether we do it consciously or not. This book helps explain how the sum of small things leads to our legacy. It demonstrates how we're also the product of the legacies we've inherited. By examining the impact our choices have on the legacy we leave, we'll learn to make wise choices.

We *will* leave a legacy, yet the question remains—Will it be the one we want?

# 2
# Deliberate LEGACIES[1]

In 1874 Richard L. Dugdale, a researcher working for the State of New York, began studying the successive generations of one family. He gave the name "Max Jukes" to the paternal head of the family and referred to the descendants as the "Jukes Family," even though the extended family consisted of people with 42 different last names.

In the late 1800s, hoping to gain more insight into Dugdale's research, new researchers compared the Jukes family with another family who lived at approximately the same time, the family of Jonathan Edwards. While both men initially seemed to have a lot in common, their legacies were ultimately very different.

## The Similarities

Max Jukes lived in New York, while Jonathan Edwards lived in Massachusetts; they both lived near woods. Though they never met, records suggest their offspring may have crossed paths.

Max loved the outdoors and considered fishing, hunting, and trapping to be his greatest skills. He made his home at the edge of a beautiful lake. There were large rocks for climbing and forests for long walks. Nature provided the privacy he needed.

Jonathan also loved nature. He often disappeared into the hills and forests near his house for a week and used the time to think through things that troubled him. He also spent a lot of time with people in his community. His fascinating personality drew people to him. When he spoke, he was graceful, natural, and earnest, and his words caused people to think. He was widely known and well liked.

Though his style of communication differed from Jonathan's, Max was also a great communicator. Before he moved to the woods, he was popular and often gathered a crowd. And though they were often vulgar, he told stories and jokes that made people laugh. His sense of humor often got him in trouble with the religious leaders of his day.

Like Max, Jonathan also got into trouble with the local religious officials, but for a different reason. One Sunday in church, Jonathan shared his opinions about the behavior of local teenagers. The prominent citizens of the town didn't like the things he said. While the adults were careful to keep their criticism quiet in public, their children directly confronted Jonathan's 11 children with accusations their parents spoke about only in whispers. For the next four years, tensions increased for the Edwards family until Jonathan was fired from his job. Those prominent citizens kicked him out of church because they disagreed with the things he said, and they ostracized Jonathan and his family to the outskirts of the civilized territory. He had no savings and no means to support his family. His wife was forced to work outside the home until handouts from friends and family arrived.

Jonathan eventually found another job, though not one as prestigious as his previous position had been. His oldest daughter grew up, married, and had two children. Then her husband suddenly passed away, and Jonathan was offered his deceased son-in-law's job. Before he could begin, however, he contracted smallpox and died. Tragically, Jonathan's wife and oldest daughter lasted only days longer before they also died of smallpox.

Of Jonathan's surviving children, six of them were under the age of 21, the youngest just 8. After both their parents, older sister, and brother-in-law were all wiped out by smallpox, the children were responsible for their niece and nephew, ages 2 and 4. The money they received after settling Jonathan's estate didn't go far.

Back in New York, Max, like Jonathan, also had a large family. He was often without a job, and he and his children took charity when it was offered. But even charity wasn't enough to provide for the family. Both Max and Jonathan died without leaving an inheritance, but the comparisons of their very different legacies continue to provide rich conversation.

## Contrasting Legacies

*The Jukes family.* Max had approximately 1,200 descendants over five generations, and researchers studied 709 of them. Out of this number were 310 paupers who required government or charitable assistance to survive. One out of every four children born into the family died during infancy from poor conditions or neglect, resulting in 300 infant deaths. Approximately 400 men and women contracted sexually transmitted diseases. Fifty women lived lives of "notorious debauchery," or prostitution. There were 140 criminals, 60 of whom were considered habitual. Seven of these were known murderers.

The traits that researchers felt best described this family were idleness, ignorance, vulgarity, and refusal to work. Many members were retarded or mentally ill. Only 20 out of the 1,200 learned a trade—10 of whom learned it in state prison—and even they did not have regular employment. The family was marked by disease, disgrace, and poverty. Researchers said that as a whole, the Jukeses were a "disgustingly diseased family"—not a legacy we would choose.

*The Edwards family.* Researchers identified over 1,300 descendants in the Edwards family. In general, they were healthy, educated, and lived long lives. From the 1,300-plus members studied, 285 graduated from college—120 from Yale alone—and many had postgraduate or professional study after college. There were approximately 100 professors and 13 presidents of colleges and universities, including Princeton and Yale. Members of Edwards's family included principals of academies and seminaries, several of which they founded. One hundred were either in the clergy, full-time missionaries, or theological professors. There were also 60 physicians and 60 prominent authors.

Many family members entered the legal profession; the family provided 100 lawyers and 30 judges and city attorneys for New York, Chicago, and Philadelphia. Eighty members of Edwards's family were elected to public office. Their elected positions included city mayors, members of both the Continental Congress and the Constitutional Conventions, a governor, several members of the United States Congress, three United States senators, one vice-president of the United States, and appointments to foreign courts. Who wouldn't be proud to be part of that family?

How can we explain the difference in the legacies of these two men whose personal lives had so many similarities?

Who were Max and Jonathan?

## Max Jukes

Max Jukes and his family settled in New York, stayed among themselves, and were even known to intermarry. Though the family contained people using 42 different last names, Max's blood flowed in each of them or his or her spouse, sometimes both. They built their homes out of stone or logs on patches of land between huge rocky clefts near the lake. In addition to shelter, those rocky clefts also provided a hiding place for the $90,000 Max's offspring had stolen from a bank.

Max's actual date of birth is unknown but is estimated to be somewhere between 1720 and 1740. He was of Dutch ancestry. Little is known about him or his childhood except what has already been mentioned; he was a popular but vulgar fellow who moved to his home in the woods near the lake so he could hide his criminal activities from the officials.

After several members of the next generation ended up in prison, Richard Dugdale, a sociologist working for the New York prisons, researched the family's origins and ultimately published his findings in their 20th annual report in 1874.

## Jonathan Edwards

Born in 1703, Jonathan Edwards was a theologian and metaphysician, someone who specializes in the branch of philosophy concerned with the study of being and beings. His ancestors were of Welsh origin and can be traced back as far as 1282. In the four generations prior to that of Jonathan were found two preachers and two merchants.

Jonathan went to college at age 12. He was an outstanding student and thinker who was extremely deliberate in his actions. While still a teenager, he wrote a series of 70 resolutions for his life. After college, he did post-graduate study, preached in New York, and tutored at Yale before joining his grandfather as co-minister in Northampton, Massachusetts. He rose every day at 4:00 A.M. and spent 13 hours a day in his study. Some of his favorite themes were predestination, absolute human dependence on God, and divine grace. When formulating a new sermon or writing, he would mount his horse and spend days riding until he had mentally worked out his argument. Then he would return home and write down the solution.

Most notably, Jonathan was responsible for a religious revival in Northampton. This particular revival is credited with beginning the Great Awakening in New England, a series of religious revivals that changed church doctrine and eventually influenced social and political thought. Stern and demanding of his congregation, one Sunday in 1750 he preached a sermon on the immoral conversations and reading material of the youth. As noted earlier, this caused a stir among several prominent citizens, many of whom had daughters who were entertaining young men late into the night—against Jonathan's advice. They called an ecclesiastical council and voted to dismiss Jonathan from his duties and to bar him from preaching or lecturing in the church again.

As mentioned previously, the family was financially unprepared for that dismissal, and Jonathan's wife was forced to work until the family received donations from friends and family. A year later, they moved to the frontier in Stockbridge, Massachusetts, to live as missionaries caring for Native Americans and ministering to a small congregation of approximately 12 white people. Jonathan did some of his best writing while in Stockbridge. There, Jonathan and his wife educated their 11 children, aged 21 to less than 1.

Approximately seven years later, one of his daughters was married to the president of Princeton when the young man died suddenly. This was the job offered to Jonathan, but he died before being able to fulfill the vacancy. His death left the family with little money—but with the knowledge that Jonathan's greatest asset was his "will," his resolution to do what was right regardless of the consequences.

## Choices

How can we explain the difference between the lives and legacies of Max Jukes and Jonathan Edwards? It's tempting to draw speculative conclusions about the role of environment, genetics, or even faith in God. There were many similarities between these two men, but we can state conclusively that Jonathan's choices and his deliberate approach to life affected his circumstances and therefore his legacy. Likewise, Max's careless and unintentional actions affected his legacy.

While we don't have the option of isolating every factor for every family, we can do this with one family in particular. In the next chapter we'll take a careful look at the "First Family." They have always lived in a fishbowl with pundits closely analyzing every move they make even years later. An examination of their choices can help us see the importance of our own decisions, just as comparing Max and Jonathan helps us to understand that the results of those choices go on for generations.

# 3
# Your CHOICES Matter

Let's look closely at the choices made by the first family—not the family of the president of the United States, although the choices made by those in office and their families are certainly interesting. The very *first* "first family" was Adam, Eve, and their sons Cain and Abel. What we learn from their choices in their primitive environment can help us understand the choices we make in what often seems a confusing world.

Things were simple for them. Adam hung out in the backyard of all backyards, the original Garden of Eden, when God gave him a job. "The LORD God took the man and put him in the Garden of Eden to work it and take care of it. And the LORD God commanded the man, 'You are free to eat from any tree in the garden; but you must not eat from the tree of the knowledge of good and evil, for when you eat of it you will surely die'" (Gen. 2:15-17).

Not many people can say they live and work in paradise. Adam's job was easy; he simply was to take care of the garden—and this was before weeds were invented!

Adam picked the ripe produce, tied up tender shoots, and made sure he got in an afternoon nap. Was Adam lonely, or did God just think Adam was having too much fun by himself? We don't know, but "The LORD God said, 'It is not good for the man to be alone. I will make a helper suitable for him'" (Gen. 2:18).

Imagine Adam's excitement. God blessed him with a helper, an attractive one too. Adam was in the middle of the garden with Eve, and together they had one obligation: to be fruitful and multiply. This was a guy who had it all: great job, good-looking wife, and a home in paradise. Of course, Eve had it pretty good, too. She was married to the richest, smartest, best-looking guy in the world, and she didn't have to do his laundry! They were human, made in God's image, with spiritual, emotional, and *rational* qualities—meaning they got to make choices too.

We already know the rest of the story. Adam and Eve chose the one thing they weren't supposed to do. They decided to eat the fruit from the tree of knowledge of good and evil. They both knew what was right, and yet they chose to do the wrong thing. Soon after this famous couple introduced original sin, they quickly followed it with original blame. When God asked Adam what he had done, Adam tried to get out of his bad decision by placing the blame on someone else: "The woman you put here with me—she gave me some fruit from the tree, and I ate it" (Gen. 3:12).

He started by blaming God and ended by blaming Eve. Not to be left out of this game, Eve passed the blame, too: "The serpent deceived me, and I ate" (v. 13). Clearly, they both knew better.

As we look back on their actions, it seems like a small choice: From which tree should they pick fruit for dinner? But this small choice had eternal consequences.

## To the Next Generation

In the previous chapter we compared Max Jukes and Jonathan Edwards and demonstrated that their choices affected their offspring. We may be tempted to attribute their differences to the environment or genetics or even dismiss them as part of a simple anecdote. But if we look at the offspring of Adam and Eve, we can't use those excuses. With an identical environment and shared genetics, Cain and Abel made separate choices that resulted in separate legacies. Their choices can't be attributed to anything but their own volition.

Cain grew crops while Abel took care of the livestock. Both were farmers doing their jobs. When it came time to bring an offering before God, Abel chose the fat portions from the firstborn of his live-stock. Unlike today, when fat is considered bad for our health, in Abel's day the fat portions were considered the very best one could offer. Abel gave God the best. So God did what we all do when we receive a nice gift—He found favor with the giver. We don't know ex-actly what Cain brought, but we know it didn't find favor with God. When Cain complained, God said, "Why are you angry? Why is your face downcast? If you do what is right, will you not be accepted? But if you do not do what is right, sin is crouching at your door; it desires to have you, but you must master it" (Gen. 4:6-7).

At that point, Cain had a choice. He could say, "You're right, God. I knew I wasn't doing what was right. I'll do better next time." He could have pulled out the choice fruits that he may have held back and said, "Here, God—here's the best fruit this land has to offer. I'm sorry I didn't give them to you first." Instead, Cain chose to kill his brother.

By removing genetics and environment as factors, the differ-ence between Cain and Abel was in the choice each of them made, or in the case of Cain, the *choices*, because he had more than one opportunity to do the right thing. Regardless of their genetics or environment, they had choices. So do we.

## On-the-Job Choices

Personal choices affect those we love and those we work with or meet casually. In some cases, we don't even need to meet some-one for our legacy to affect him or her. Need proof? Look at the business failures in the beginning of this century.

Enron was a company that experienced unbelievable growth in what has traditionally been a slow-growth market. At its peak in 2000, it reported revenue of $101 billion. If we wrote a check out for this amount—$101,000,000,000—the zeros wouldn't fit. Enron had stakes in nearly 30,000 miles of gas pipeline, a 15,000-mile fiber op-tic network, and electricity-generating operations worldwide.

So how does a company with real assets, significant revenues, and thousands of employees go broke? Poor choices.

Executives made poor choices on leadership, growth strate-gies, financial accounting, and integrity. As much as former employees, shareholders, and the media would like to blame a single executive, there was an environment that allowed many people to make poor choices. We all adapt to the environment we're in. If we're in a company that takes integrity lightly, then we will, too. If this is allowed to continue, it's like the adage about slowly raising the heat on a frog in a pan of water. The frog doesn't realize it's getting hotter until he's almost cooked.

What happened when the executives were caught and brought to court? Their defense was the oldest defense in the world: "Uh, it's not my fault—he made me do it," blaming various levels of management—anyone but themselves. The employees who lost their jobs were the ones who absorbed the brunt of the consequences of the executives' behavior, but ripples went on to people the executives never even met, specifically to employees' spouses and children. The entire community suffered financial losses as tax revenues and donations to arts organizations and other community-supported non-profit groups dropped dramatically.

Consider another example of how seemingly insignificant choices affect even our casual contacts. Martha Stewart is the domestic diva who took a small catering business and grew it into a billion-dollar company that included magazines, television shows, and branded products. Her niche market became an entire industry, drawing in a sort of cult-like following among suburban moms that hasn't been seen since the minivan. Yet that success didn't stop the accusations made against her of selling stock based upon insider information. She, of course, denied it. What's interesting to note is that the money she made on the alleged transaction—her financial gain—was less than she could have made selling a few towels at K-mart or creating a new ham glaze. But rather than absorb a relatively small loss and admit what she did, Martha lied about her actions, according to allegations. The court found her guilty.

As a result of her cover-up, she was convicted of conspiracy and obstruction of justice, her net worth dropped by 50 percent, she spent time in prison, and she lost control of her own company. Obviously, her choices affected her and her legacy, but they also affected the millions of consumers who trusted her products, the people who manufactured and sold her branded items, and the employees of her companies.

In the Enron and Martha Stewart cases, we're not talking about one bad decision. We're talking about progressively worse infractions that resulted in lost jobs for employees, foreclosures due to missed mortgage payments, and for those who had difficulty getting new jobs, a lack of health insurance. But these aren't the only examples of corporate scandal: think of Tyco, WorldCom, Global Crossing, and Health South.

Imagine how things could have turned out differently if any of those companies had had executives who were concerned about their legacies and about how their choices affected others. They might have acted like Sharon Watkins. She's the Enron employee who put her reputation and job on the line to raise questions and concerns to the board of directors and CEO about some of Enron's accounting practices. Was this an easy choice for her to make? There must have been many sleepless nights preceding an action like hers. *Should I say something or not? Is this really an issue worth bringing up? Maybe I should just act as if I don't see anything.* Undoubtedly, she suffered for the choices she made, but her legacy will be a very different one than that of her employers.

## It's Your Choice

Good choices result from people who understand that their actions have significance and that their choices have consequences beyond what they can see. Bad choices result from those who don't see that they have a choice. When faced with the consequences of their bad decisions, they claim that there wasn't a decision, they had no choice, or the blame belongs to someone else.

To make good decisions, we need to take responsibility for our choices. We can say all the right things, but unless we carry out the steps to make it happen, we haven't really made a decision that lasts. Our actions speak louder than our words, and our intentional actions speak for generations. Are we willing to assign to ourselves the task of being intentional in the decisions we make?

# 4
# Seemingly
# Insignificant
# DETAILS

Richard Carlson wrote *Don't Sweat the Small Stuff . . . and It's All Small Stuff.* The book suggests that you shouldn't worry about seemingly small things. Some may take this a step further and conclude that the small stuff isn't important. Maybe they believe that some choices are life-altering but only the big ones, like where we go to college, what we major in, the first job we accept, the spouse we choose, and where we live really matter.

Maybe they don't believe that every choice can permanently alter a legacy. Are we unconvinced that small stuff matters? Do we believe arbitrary decisions such as when to take a fishing trip, where to meet a client, or whether to leave work early for a family function make a difference? Do we believe that inconsequential details of life are inconsequential to our legacy?

## Details, Details

Consider the insignificant choices these people made.

- The weather is supposed to be perfect. Joe, Matt, and three of their coworkers decide to take a few days off work and go on their annual fishing trip. It means time away from their family and work that accumulates while they're gone, but they all agree that the trip will be worth it.
- David's clients call from the lobby. One of them doesn't have the proper ID. To get the clients into his office, either David

or his assistant has to take the elevator down from his high-rise office and escort the clients through security. He looks at his assistant; she's on the phone and she's also seven months pregnant. Should he go down and let them in, or should he ask her to do it?

- Stephen decides to stop by the gym on his way to the office to ask about an exercise plan. A tourist stops him and asks for directions. Stephen realizes he will now be a few minutes late to the office but decides to stop by the gym anyway.

- Howard is a hard-charging executive of one of the largest financial companies in the world. But on one particular morning, he chooses to go to work late so that he can take his son Kyle to school for his first day of kindergarten.

- Family is a priority to Doug, and it's a busy week for his family with his father's birthday and with two kids starting back to school. He postpones his business trip until the following week to meet his family's needs. Doug goes into the office early Tuesday so he can leave by 5:00; he and his family will celebrate his dad's birthday at a local restaurant.

These decisions seem insignificant, and they appear to have little impact on the person's legacy. We make the same, or similar choices, several times a day. In fact, we probably make daily decisions that have much bigger consequences than these.

Joe, Matt, David, Stephen, and Howard made choices on Tuesday, September 11, 2001, that saved their lives.

If Joe and Matt hadn't been on a fishing trip, if Stephen hadn't stopped to give directions to a tourist and then gone by the gym, if David had sent his assistant downstairs instead of going himself, and if Howard had missed his son's first day of school, each very possibly would have died in the terrorist attack on the World Trade Center in New York City. But because of the seemingly inconsequential details of their lives on that day, those Cantor-Fitzgerald employees are all alive, while 658 of their coworkers are dead.[1]

It would be easy to conclude that David, Howard, and the others made the *right* choices, but Doug did all the right things too. He cancelled a business trip to be home with his family. He went in to work early to meet his business obligations and still leave in time to celebrate his dad's birthday. Doug didn't make the wrong choices, but his choices resulted in his death.

Whether their choices were right or wrong isn't the issue. The point is this: the small things, the seemingly inconsequential things we choose to do, make a difference.

## God Is in the Details

Our God is a God of small stuff. If we've been driving for a number of years, chances are that we don't think twice about the dead animals lying in the road as we drive by. There are even T-shirts and bumper stickers making fun of "roadkill." Sure, an occasional dog or cat that was obviously someone's pet will get our attention, but have we ever mourned a possum or a squirrel? When was the last time we noticed a dead bird?

Jesus tried to explain to the religious leaders that the God they feared because of His awesome power—*that same God*—also cares about the smallest details like dead birds along the road. "Are not two sparrows sold for a penny? Yet not one of them will fall to the ground apart from the will of your Father" (Matt. 10:29).

Jesus reminds us that God cares about us, that He cares about the details of our lives. "Even the very hairs of your head are all numbered. So don't be afraid; you are worth more than many sparrows" (Matt. 10:30-31). The hairs we wash down the shower drain, the birds alongside the road—those are important details to God. A well-known expression says, "The devil is in the details," but the truth is that God is in the details. He was in the small stuff of the people who lived September 11, and not one of those who died on that day did so apart from His will.

That's a strong statement; let's make sure we understand what it means. A bunch of terrorists kill innocent people, and we claim that God wanted it? No!

No one said that God *wanted* it or even that He *willed* it. But if the verse above says that not even a sparrow will fall to the ground apart from the will of the Father, then it's safe to assume that things can't happen *apart from His will*. God knew what was happening, and He was there.

This is a tough subject. Philosophers and theologians much

greater than the authors of this book have wrestled with this issue. There's a lot of good evidence on all sides of the providence
issue historically and denominationally, and we're not sure we understand it all. But what we're saying transcends our personal beliefs, and we hope yours as well. Regardless of whether we believe
in predestination, pre-Tribulation or post-Tribulation rapture,
God is in the details, and sometimes bad things happen under His
control. We can all agree on that. Yet we often act as though bad
things take away the ability to make positive choices.

For example, a sick person might say, "Well, you would be bitter, too, if you had cancer." Many people would be. But cancer
doesn't take away the choice to be happy or to live life positively.
Cancer provides us with an acceptable rationale to be bitter or
angry or whatever we want an excuse to feel. But if God is in the
details—the smallest details of the choices we make—even bad
things happening around us (or to us) can't be reason enough to
choose to do the wrong thing.

Right after Jesus tells us that God cares about the little things
—like sparrows and hairs on our head—He tells us that we have a
choice to make: "Whoever acknowledges me before men, I will also acknowledge him before my Father in heaven. But whoever
disowns me before men, I will disown him before my Father in
heaven" (Matt. 10:32-33).

There isn't anything ambiguous here. Jesus tells us that He
cares about the smallest details in our lives and then asks *us* to
make a choice. This also seems like a pretty insignificant choice:
You can acknowledge Jesus or choose to disown Him. Don't be
fooled. This could be the most important decision you ever make.

Our choices matter. We already knew the big ones did. Maybe
now we can understand how the small stuff also matters. What we
say, how we say it, and from which tree we pick our fruit matters
to us and to the legacy we leave.

What choices will you make?

# 5
# To the FOURTH Generation

We didn't make up the title of this chapter. We took it right out of the Word—the Bible. It comes from the second part of Exod. 20:5. Exodus has a lot to say about passing on a legacy. The book begins with the Israelites in captivity in Egypt. God works miracles through Moses, who leads them out of slavery. Three months after the Israelites leave Egypt, Moses takes them to the Desert of Sinai, where they camp in front of the holy mountain, Mt. Sinai. God calls Moses up the mountain and gives him the Ten Commandments, the second of which forbids making idols. (Exod. 20:4). God warns the Israelites, "You shall not bow down to them or worship them; for I, the LORD your God, am a jealous God, punishing the children for the sin of the fathers to the third and fourth generation of those who hate me" (v. 5).

Maybe this verse doesn't concern us. We're not idolaters, and we don't come from a family of idolaters. No one in our houses makes statues of calves or bulls out of gold. Why *would* God be jealous? Why would someone hate God anyway?

## God Is Jealous?

When we hear the word "jealous," we think of the envious, suspicious, distrustful feelings we have about the success of others. We're tempted to think God might have the same kinds of emotions. But when God says He is a jealous God, He isn't envious of a bull made out of gold or any other inanimate object we create. Our creations pose no threat to Him. He isn't after our objects—He's after our attention.

God zealously seeks our devotion. He protects us when He says not to worship idols. He knows the things of this world easily distract us. God demands our exclusive dedication. If anything in our lives competes with the honor and glory that is due Him, He is righteously angry—that is, He is jealous.

Consider the Israelites. They would capture a land, and before they knew it they were worshiping foreign gods. While they believed the God of Israel was the one true God, their behavior indicated otherwise as time and again they began following false gods. In the beginning it was just a little going astray, but eventually it was to the exclusion of Jehovah. Perhaps at first it was a sort of "other-god insurance policy," but before long it was all-out devotion to other deities.

Parents used to use the phrase "You'd better dance with the one who brought you" to admonish daughters who were happy to have a less-than-desirable date take them to a dance, hoping to upgrade once they got there. We need to realize that God is the one who brought us to the dance and that He is our perfect partner. When we choose to dance with another or become distracted by something else, God's jealousy isn't caused by insecurity. He's not jealous of our new dance partner. His jealousy flows from His love for us. God knows that any other dance partner is hazardous to our being. He is fiercely protective of us and wants only what's best for us. It makes Him angry to see us turn toward something that is not good for us. Of course, anything that isn't of God isn't good.

His jealousy is not the envious, emotional experience we have; rather, it is His zealous attachment to us—seeking our return to Him. What an awesome thing to be loved so dearly!

So the question becomes this: What is distracting you from God? Maybe you're not making idols in the biblical sense. But is your devotion to God distracted by financial pressures, self-promotion, relationships that have soured, lack of time, or the need to get ahead? In the morning, do you have quiet time with the sports page or with a page of the Bible?

We may not worship baby cows made of gold, but our culture is certainly still in the business of idolatry. We make idols of movie actors, musicians, and athletes. We also worship things closer to home, such as our own children or even sleep.

It's easy to overlook the idols we've built when they've taken such a hold on our lives. We no longer see them as a distraction from God, because they actually block our view of God. If we become conscious of our behavior, we immediately dismiss it. We ask ourselves, *Why would God be jealous about such petty things?*—a further indication that we've already blocked Him out.

## Those Who Hate God

Exod. 5:20 contains another strong emotional word—"hate." God says He'll punish the future generations of those who hate Him. Yes, we've sinned—but that doesn't mean we *hate* God, does it?

Just as God's jealousy is different from our green-eyed emotional experience, the hate that God refers to is different. When God talks about hate, He refers not to passionate dislike but rather an absence of love—often manifested in a lack of obedience.[1] Therefore, in God's terms, to disobey is to hate.

We've already established that we can be idolaters, choosing to involve ourselves with people or things that distract us from God. It's obvious that we don't always obey Him, so by definition we sometimes hate Him.

We have one more piece of bad news to deliver before we get to the good news. Not only are we idolaters and God-haters before we come to Him, deserving of punishment, but God says we'll also be punished for the sins of our fathers for up to four generations: "Punishing the children for the sin of the fathers to the third and fourth generation of those who hate me" (Exod. 20:5).

## Punishing the Children

It's one thing to be punished for our own sins, but for the sins of our fathers? That doesn't seem fair, does it? But that's what the verse clearly says—it's repeated in Exod. 34:7; Num. 14:18; and Deut. 5:9. However, those verses demonstrate why we need to study Scripture in context. While the verse clearly says that God will punish children for the sins of their fathers, there isn't an example of that happening in the Bible.

Some cite the story of Achan as an example of a family punished for the sins of one member. In this story from Josh. 7, Achan, a member of the tribe of Judah, kept some of the spoils of war after the Israelites' victory over Jericho, despite God's (and Joshua's) warnings not to take anything. When confronted, Achan confessed, and he and his family were stoned to death.

However, biblical scholars argue this is not a case of an innocent family unjustly punished. Achan had taken treasures and buried them under the family tent. He could not have done this without the knowledge (and some biblical scholars say, approval) of his family; therefore, they were complicit in his sin. Furthermore, when they had an opportunity to acknowledge their sin, they didn't speak up. Only after Achan was found guilty did he confess. Scholars believe Achan's family members were punished not for his sins but their own.[2]

While this may be an anecdotal case, Scripture directly supports the view that individuals are punished for their own sin, not for someone else's. For example, "Fathers shall not be put to death for their children, nor children put to death for their fathers; each is to die for his own sin" (Deut. 24:16).

Ezek. 18 is devoted to the issue of who gets punished for whose sin. This is a chapter we can all relate to. It introduces the subject of accountability, and every possible variation of the subject is discussed. Some of the same questions you're asking right now are probably answered in that chapter.

In verse 4 it's clear that "the soul who sins is the one who will die." Or as a modern prophet might say, "If *you* do the crime, *you* do the time." But in verses 5-9, for those who still have questions, Ezekiel lays it out in a detailed "what if?" scenario. What if a person is good and does what's right? What if he or she isn't an idolater or an adulterer? What if the person pays his or her bills, doesn't steal, gives food to the hungry, is honest in his or her business dealings, judges fairly, and obeys God's laws? As expected, the Lord says that person is righteous and will live.

Another "what if?" or "yeah, but" question is asked in the following verses. What if the person has a son, and that son isn't so good? What if the son is violent, maybe kills people, commits adultery, steals, mistreats the poor, and does other detestable things? Again, the answer is what we would expect. In verse 13 the Lord says that such a man will not live, but he will be put to death, and his blood will be on his own head.

A question remains: What if the bad son has a good son? What, then? Is the good son punished for his father's sins? Ezekiel makes the answer very clear, starting in verse 17:

> He will not die for his father's sin; he will surely live. But his father will die for his own sin, because he practiced extortion, robbed his brother and did what was wrong among his people.
>
> Yet you ask, "Why does the son not share the guilt of his father?" Since the son has done what is just and right and has been careful to keep all my decrees, he will surely live. The soul who sins is the one who will die. The son will not share the guilt of the father, nor will the father share the guilt of the son. The righteousness of the righteous man will be credited to him, and the wickedness of the wicked will be charged against him (*Ezek. 18:17-20*).

Taking this extended look at scripture, it's clear that we aren't punished for the sins of our fathers, yet in the verses we looked at in the beginning of this chapter, it clearly says that the punishment for the sins of the father goes on to the fourth generation. How do we make sense of that?

## The Consequences of Sin

Unlike in today's society, in which grandparents are often separated from their families by considerable distances, in biblical times households typically contained several generations. The actions of all family members affected the whole family because of their proximity to and their dependence on each other.

Think of it this way. If while you were growing up your father drove drunk and killed another driver, you would not be sent to jail. Your father would. However, the loss of his income, the guilt your family would feel, and the stress your mother would suffer while negotiating all the financial and legal ramifications would definitely affect you and your siblings. The same was true in biblical days.

The best understanding of the verses that talk about punishment to the third and fourth generation is that the guilty person's actions have consequences, and these consequences will reverberate throughout the family for up to four generations (the presumed upper limit of a lifespan). Thus, while the sinner alone is responsible for his or her actions, the family must share in the consequences.

## The Good News

If we combine everything we've looked at so far in this chapter, it's easy to see that before we come to Christ, we're all idolaters and God-haters. Or let's simply say it—sinners. We all deserve punishment before we bow before Him in repentance. We also understand that while our children aren't directly punished for our actions, they will feel the consequences from our behavior for up to four generations. By extension, we can assume our choices can also affect our friends, coworkers, neighbors, and even our churches for generations.

Just as the choices made by Max Jukes and Jonathan Edwards, or even Adam and Eve, affected their families, the choices we make will continue to affect our loved ones.

How should we choose to live our lives?

In the next several chapters we'll try to understand and make deliberate choices about the small details in our lives, because ultimately the sum of our small choices will be the legacy we leave —to the fourth generation.

# part 2

## The Legacy We Leave

*The best inheritance a parent can give his children
is a few minutes of his time each day.*
—O. A. Battista

*Property left to a child may soon be lost; but the inheritance of
virtue—a good name an unblemished reputation—will abide forever.
If those who are toiling for wealth to leave their children would but
take half the pains to secure for them virtuous habits, how much
more serviceable would they be. The largest property may be
wrested from a child, but virtue will stand by him to the last.*
—William Graham Sumner (1840-1910)

*No legacy is so rich as honesty.*
—William Shakespeare (1564-1616)

*We are all gifted. That is our inheritance.*
—Ethel Waters

*Live such good lives among the pagans that, though they
accuse you of doing wrong, they may see your good deeds
and glorify God on the day he visits us.*
—1 Pet. 2:12

# 6
# Minutes
## Make a
# DIFFERENCE

For each day he's in office, the president of the United States gets 1,440. After he leaves office, he will continue to get that much each day *for the rest of his life*. The authors of this book will each get 525,600 this year. Bill Gates will spend over 40 million if he lives an average lifespan. How many do you have, and how will you spend yours?

These numbers don't represent dollars—they represent the number of minutes each of us has to spend in a day, a year, and over an average lifetime. Some of us try to hide certain numbers, like those of our ages, weight, or bank accounts. These numbers are personal and vary according to each individual, but there are other numbers we all hold in common. We each have 1,440 minutes in a day. In a year we have 525,600, and if we live to the age of 77 (the average lifespan), we'll have had over 40 million minutes to spend! How we spend—or waste—a minute seems insignificant until we realize that, unlike money, once we've spent our minutes, we can't earn more. Further complicating things is that while we all have the same number of minutes per day, we're not guaranteed to have the same number of days on earth, so the best we can hope for is to wisely spend the minutes we're given today.

That's because the undisputable fact is that time is a precious commodity. It is a limited resource. When it's lost, we can't find more of it. Whether we actively spend it or passively pass it, once it's gone we can't reclaim it. We can't manufacture more of it, and we can't buy it.

A glance around will reveal marketers trying to persuade us differently. In Jennifer's office is a magazine that promises "Time for Yourself: Where to Find It, How to Keep It." In her kitchen are cookbooks that promise balanced and healthful meals in minutes. Her Internet provider promises the fastest download speeds possible so she can spend less time surfing the web. Each of these items has an implicit promise: "We can give you more time."

Why do we spend money on things that we know can't give us what they promise? We do this because we all know people who seem to get everything done and still have time left over, and we want to be like them. So the question really is *How do they do it?*

## Multi-tasking Mania

In our time-conscious, success-oriented, hyper-speed culture, one way to beat the clock is to do more than one thing at a time. Until recently, women have held all the gold medals in this competition. In the morning they can dry their hair, put on makeup, get dressed, get the kids dressed, feed the family breakfast, sign yesterday's homework, feed the dog, make lunches, throw in a load of laundry, and start thawing supper all at the same time.

It's likely they'll be able to do even more in the future as new technologies are helping microwaves to toast, washers to dry, and ovens to keep dinner safely cold until it's time to cook. In many cases, this is good. Occasionally, it's not. Craig once got rear-ended by a multi-tasking maven who was trying to apply eyeliner and drive at the same time.

Technology is also helping business people do more at once. A high-tech tool has replaced the pocket watch. It may be a cell phone, Blackberry, or a PDA (personal data assistant). These technological wonders of multi-tasking do more than just tell time—they allow us to have conversations with anyone at any time. Clients can now reach us anywhere, even on vacation. We can store our calendars, address books, to-do lists, and favorite reading material. Why carry a camera when we can snap photos with our phone? We no longer have to sit at a desk to download e-mail or surf the web; now we can do it at the dinner table, in traffic, or even in bed.

Technology can be good, and doing more than one thing at a time can often help us redeem time that we would otherwise spend doing mundane chores. But when technology steals time from relationships, or multi-tasking means never having to sit still and listen, something is wrong with our outlook—our view on life, not the Microsoft product by the same name.

Many years ago Jennifer sold computers based on the sales pitch that they would save her clients time. Now we *waste* more time solving fatal errors, deleting unwanted e-mails, and holding for customer "no-support" than we ever dreamed of *saving*. To make up for the time we've wasted, we spend more time on the computer, sometimes at the expense of our relationships. Daytime talk shows are filled with stories and statistics of people who cheat on their spouses. Yet every day, well-meaning couples with seemingly good relationships are separated not by lap dances but by laptops when one partner tries to squeeze a little more work out of the day by bringing technology into the bedroom.

We may be responsible parents who set limits on how long our kids use the computer or television. But are we equally responsible when it comes to *our* use of media? Or do we spend time on the computer when we could be spending time with our spouses and our kids? Experts recommend that kids get no more than an hour of media per day, believing that they should instead spend their time playing and developing relationships. Parents often agree, complaining that their children spend too much time playing video games or watching television, and they try to control it by setting limits. Yet some of these parents are the same ones who talk on their cell phones rather than talk with their children. When we look at our cell phone bills, how many minutes did we spend on it last month?

We're not pointing fingers at the worst offenders, people who truly don't care about their kids or those who are using the computer for illicit viewing. We're talking about people like us, well-meaning moms and dads who sometimes forget what's most important in the presence of what's most urgent.

## Bill's Story

For most of us, our family is important, but work often becomes urgent. That's what happened to our friend Bill. An accountant with lots of initials after his name (CPA, CFP, PFS, and CLU), Bill is someone clients trust to be a good steward of their money. He has a wonderful wife and four small children. To meet his financial goals, Bill has had some aggressive expectations of himself at work. He has put in long hours, not a hard thing to do when he enjoys his work and has a supportive spouse.

One day a friend who noticed Bill's ever-increasing schedule asked him some hard questions, beginning with "How many nights do you make it home for dinner?"

Bill thought about it and realized he missed an average of four out of five nights each week. Then the friend asked another question.

"Do you have a faith issue regarding work?"

The friend knew Bill was a Christian and that he professed that God came first in his life, but when it came time to prove himself at work, Bill used his own strength to muscle his way through the day.

God used the friend to show Bill that there wasn't anything wrong with his goals but there was something wrong with the way he set about accomplishing them. We can all work longer to accomplish our goals, but do we trust God enough to get it done in the time we have?

That conversation affected Bill, and he changed the way he scheduled his time. Now dinner, not work, is an appointment he doesn't miss. He also accomplishes all his goals at work, and his family is happier. For him, it wasn't a time issue but a faith issue about how he used his time. If your legacy is important to you, look through the eyes of others at how you spend your time. Bill's friend saw things differently than Bill did.

Perhaps the best way to get a fresh perspective on life is to look at the things we do through the eyes of our children. Do we want our teenage daughter on the cell phone at the dinner table or while she's driving? If we don't want *her* to do it, we shouldn't model that behavior ourselves. When our kids have a question about sex, drugs, or alcohol, would we prefer that they talk to us or talk to a friend? Openly talking about things as a family will do a lot to cut down on questions kids might otherwise ask outside the family. But the way to develop the kind of trust we need for those discussions to take place is to be there. It won't be long before a teenager is grown and married, and when that happens, would we prefer that he or she spend time in bed with a laptop, or talk and listen to his or her spouse? If we believe relationships are important to our children's lives, we need to teach them to relate to people, not to technology.

Like the Harry Chapin song suggests, our kids are learning to be just like us. Are we spending our minutes the way we want them to spend theirs?

## Priorities

Suppose we listed our priorities. Most people would say family or job is their first priority. If we're people of faith, we might say it's God or church. After that, our list might include things like health or fitness-related activities. Maybe we have volunteer commitments, hobbies, or community-related obligations. That's good. Those are the right answers—the things we're supposed to say.

If we can't list our priorities off the top of our heads, we need to spend a few minutes thinking through them. Once we have a mental or written picture of our priorities, we can compare that with how we actually spend our time each day.

What do we spend the majority of our day doing? It's probably some kind of work—either a job or chores around the house. Our next block of time might be commuting or watching television. Maybe it's exercising. If we're home before the kids go to bed, hopefully we spend time with the family at dinner. Afterward, we're probably pursuing our own things in separate rooms.

Do we see how most of the day isn't spent on the things that are our highest priorities? Think of it this way: If each of our priorities was a jar and all our minutes were marbles, would the biggest jars contain the most marbles? Or would smaller, less important jars overflow with marbles?

## How Do We Spend Our Minutes?

Warehouse clubs often sell oversized jars of pickles. Those things could hold hundreds, maybe thousands, of marbles or, for the sake of our example, minutes. What label would we put on such a big jar? Based on our discussion above, it's probably God, family, or maybe job. Now think of the tiny, one-sized serving jar of baby food. At most, one might hold 30 marbles, representing enough minutes to read the newspaper or watch the 6:00 news.

Somewhere in our lives is a peanut butter jar labeled for time spent exercising or doing a hobby. In a balanced life, all the jars are filled according to size, none left overflowing and none left empty. This is the legacy we desire to leave, a life that's balanced according to our priorities.

How do your jars measure up?

Maybe we said family was high on our priority list—it's a big jar. Our job is also important, but it's not our first priority, so that container isn't quite as big. As we spend time at the office, do paperwork at home, or have cell phone conversations with clients, we keep dropping marbles into the jar labeled "work." The time we spend eating dinner with the kids, helping with homework, and tucking them into bed results in marbles in the "family" jar.

When we stop to count our marbles, does the large family jar have more or fewer marbles than the work jar? For many, it seems as if all the marbles (or minutes) that belong to the family somehow keep ending up in the jar labeled "Work."

If faith is important to us, we might have a gigantic "God" jar. If we toss up only a few quick prayers and spend a few seconds reading a devotional during the day, we won't have enough marbles to cover the bottom of the jar, let alone fill it. Either time or the investment in spiritual growth or both must increase if faith is really important to us.

Leaving a legacy isn't simply about parking our marbles in the correct jar, and this isn't a guilt trip for those occasional times when you need to work a few extra hours. Leaving a legacy is about finding a balance between priorities and the amount of time you spend on them. If you say your marriage is a priority but you don't spend time with your spouse—is it really your priority?

Priority implies the importance of one thing over another. Your family and your job can't be equal priorities. If your child becomes critically injured while you're at a company picnic, you wouldn't think twice about leaving the picnic for the hospital. You would run with your child to the car. When it really counts, family is your first priority.

Maybe there are seasons in life or times of the year when your job requires more time or attention. If you work in retail, your hours increase during the holidays; if you're a CPA, for a few months out of every year work takes on greater importance; and if you're a writer on deadline, you may grow increasingly stressed as the date draws near. Thankfully for us, our families understand the need to accommodate our writing schedules, but since we're both married to CPAs, we also know that there are seasons when we have to take on more responsibility at home while they focus on their jobs too.

In both cases, it doesn't mean work is a greater priority than family. What it means is taking the time to sit down with our loved ones and ask them to step up and temporarily fill roles we normally fill at home, but to do it just for a season.

If family is our priority, we seek their help in working out our need to spend more time or focus on our jobs. We make it only a period of time, not a way of life. It also means we need to take time to reflect and make sure we prioritize our time correctly and, like Bill, learn to depend on God for help in getting it all done.

When articles or books promise to help us save time, they aren't actually showing us where to shop for more minutes. What they're demonstrating is how to move our marbles from jars we don't like, such as meetings or cleaning the oven, into jars that align with our desires and priorities, such as playing golf or spending time with the family. While balance between time and priorities is a worthy goal, ultimately we still have only 1,440 minutes of time to spend each day.

We would all like to control time to our advantage, but the only control we have is how we spend the time we're given. Our best choice is to know our priorities and divide our time according to those priorities. If something unexpected comes up, we need to be flexible enough to adjust our schedules by getting approval from the people who are our first priority. Like Bill, we need to make sure that it isn't a faith issue, but we trust God to help us get done what He's given us to do. Bill says that he was fortunate to have a friend to ask him the hard questions.

We must investigate whether we balance our time and priorities in a way that will help us create a positive legacy. If we need help seeing how well we manage our time in light of our priorities, we must ask those whom we consider a priority. Next time you pray, ask God if you're using your time wisely. Ask your spouse if he or she feels like a priority. But be prepared! What you learn may improve your spiritual life and your marriage if you act on the feedback you receive. Better yet, ask your kids. They're so honest that you might be shocked by the disconnect they see between your words and how you actually spend your time.

Most of us don't have the amount of money to pass on to our children that Bill Gates has to pass on to his. We may not be the president of a company, but time is the great equalizer. We get the same amount each day that everyone else gets, but we get to choose how we'll use it.

It may not be practical to spend every day as if it held our last 1,440 minutes, but we can use each minute in such a way that if it's our last, we'll be proud of how we spent it. A life of well-spent minutes is a legacy worth leaving.

# 7

# INDEBTED

Whom Do We Owe?

There are many ways for a church to spend money, but giving it back to the people who donated it is one of the most unusual. When Pastor Denny Bellesi of Coast Hills Community Church in Aliso Viejo, California, handed out $100 bills to 100 members of his congregation, the reactions were mixed. Denny's wife, Leesa, remembers, "Initially most of them were shocked. They were in church, and he was handing them money. They were holding it up to be sure it was real."[1]

## Modern Parable of Talents

On that Sunday, Pastor Bellesi preached a sermon from Matt. 25:14-30 about the parable of the talents. In it, Jesus tells the story of a man who gives money to his three servants before he leaves on a trip. To the first he gives five talents, to the second he gives three, and to the third he gives one. Each talent is approximately the equivalent of 20 years' worth of wages—a very significant amount of money. Roughly speaking, that would be between $300,000 to $600,000 per talent, meaning that the servant who got five talents received the equivalent of several million dollars.

When the master returns, he finds that the first two servants have doubled the money they were given—a considerable accomplishment. The master is pleased and promises to entrust more to both.

When the third servant comes forth, he returns the talent he was given and nothing more. The servant tells his master that he was afraid and so he dug a hole to keep the money safe. The master is upset that the servant hasn't handled the money entrusted to him more wisely. At the very least, he informs the servant, he could have put the talent in the bank and earned interest on the money. The master takes the talent from him and gives it to the first servant. He reprimands the third servant, saying, "For everyone who has will be given more, and he will have an abundance. Whoever does not have, even what he has will be taken from him. And throw that worthless servant outside, into the darkness, where there will be weeping and gnashing of teeth" (Matt. 25:29-30).

With the backdrop of Jesus' teaching, Pastor Bellesi asked for 100 volunteers, and they each stood on stage holding his or her 100-dollar bill. Most were confused until Bellesi outlined the rules for them. They were to acknowledge that the money was God's, not theirs; they were to use it for God outside the church, and in 90 days they were to report what happened.

Some tried to give the money back. Others cried. A few were angry and frustrated. Most were concerned about taking money *from* the church; they were used to *giving* money. However, they didn't have the option of giving it back.

Their initial shock gave way to fear. "One man wanted to give the money to the first homeless person he saw," recalls Leesa. "But most of them left the church that day thinking it was the most important $100 they ever held."

The following Sunday, other members who hadn't volunteered returned to the church and said, "I would have volunteered if I had known you were going to give me $100."

This is when many preachers would have said it wasn't too late and asked members to take $100 of their own money and do the same thing. Bellesi explained that we all have that much money or more every month, and it's not just the 100-dollar bills he handed out that belong to God—it *all* belongs to Him.

## Who Owns It?

"Wait a minute!" you might say skeptically. "I've worked hard for what I have. No one just gave it to me—I earned it."

Maybe you can follow up such a statement with legitimate claims such as you worked to pay for school or advanced from the mailroom to the boardroom. Maybe you managed your money through the early years so you would have extra for retirement. Perhaps you worked and built your business from nothing. Those are all good things, and you should be proud of your accomplishments. However, despite your success, you didn't do it alone.

If we were pressed, we would probably admit that we couldn't be the person we are or be in the position we're in without the help, influence, teaching, mentoring, coaching, and guidance of others. If those people contributed to our success, don't we owe them? While we may have been the driver behind our good fortune, we didn't do it alone. Someone or something extra played a part. We can call it what we will—good fortune, good decisions, or personal strength— but the Bible says that the something extra is God.

> For everything in heaven and earth is yours. Yours, O LORD, is the kingdom; you are exalted as head over all. Wealth and honor come from you; you are the ruler of all things. In your hands are strength and power to exalt and give strength to all (*1 Chron. 29:11-12*).

Everything comes from God—your talent, your time, your wealth, and as the verses above say, even your strength and power. That means you didn't even get out of bed this morning on your own—God gave you the strength to do that. These verses couldn't make it clearer: absolutely *everything* comes from God. It's His, given to us, to use for Him.

How does that change the way we handle money?

When the term "stewardship" is used in church, many believe that it means the preacher is getting ready to ask for money. But being a steward isn't something we do only on Sundays. "Steward" means a manager, someone who manages property, finances, or affairs for the owner. An employee is a steward of the business he or she works for; he or she is responsible for using the company resources wisely to fulfill the corporate mission and to make a profit. We might be stewards for our aging parents, trying to manage their resources so that they'll have the care they need until they die. As parents, we steward our resources to meet our children's needs for food, shelter, and education.

A good steward needs to be a meticulous money manager who carefully invests what is given to him or her in order to ensure the best return for his or her client. A steward shares the same burden as a trustee except that the ramifications are spiritual rather than legal. "Moreover it is required in stewards, that a man be found faithful" (1 Cor. 4:2, KJV). Characteristics discussed later such as integrity and fidelity are key to being good stewards. Stewards have responsibilities—it's where the legacy we talk meets our walk.

## The Weight of Responsibility

What happened to the stewards at Bellesi's church? The church members took their responsibility seriously. One woman invested in paper and made custom-designed stationery that she sold in local gift stores, more than doubling her original investment. She donated all the money to charity. Another man wrote to his fraternity brothers and told them about the challenge. He wanted to use his money to help a family with three very sick children. For every dollar they donated, he matched it. Most of his fraternity brothers didn't know he went to church, but they helped him raise $8,000 to cover the funeral costs of two of the children. A doctor who likes to surf in exotic locations received $100 and used it to apply for a grant that eventually resulted in a medical clinic in Indonesia.

Teri Zwick prayed about opening a shelter for abused women. She asked a few friends to invest with her in helping a woman and her children who were in need of the basic necessities of life. As others learned of her passion, they also wanted to contribute. Eventually, Teri raised enough to open a shelter called Hope's House in a home near the beach. The total cost of the property and furnishings came to more than a million dollars—completely donated by people who wanted to help.

Imagine what a church full of 100-dollar bills could do! But God doesn't want us to manage a 100-dollar bill as if it were the most important money we ever received. He wants us to manage *everything we have*, just as those members managed their $100.

## A Loose Grip, Not Loose Change

"Everything comes from you, and we have given you only what comes from your hand" (1 Chron. 29:14).

The members at Bellesi's church were eager to give away their 100-dollar bills because they never took mental ownership of them. But if we feel the money is ours, it's harder for us to part with it. Think of someone dropping a 100-dollar bill while we stand behind him or her in line at the bank. There's no question about picking it up and returning it to its rightful owner. But if I pick up my own 100-dollar bill and the person ahead of me claims he or she needs it for an emergency, I'm not likely to hand it over —at least not without a few questions.

When we let go of ownership, or rather we correctly assign ownership to God, giving becomes very easy. This is more than an intellectual exercise where we think about God being in control; we need to be able to give it all to Him, physically as well as emotionally. Let it go. God doesn't need our money—He requires our compliance. We can't be obedient unless we acknowledge that He owns everything, and it's the owner who decides how the resources should be used.

Without understanding that all we have is God's and we're to use what He's given us for His purposes, we become like addicts chasing the next high. No amount of money will ever satisfy. While the church members felt a great weight of responsibility when given the $100, they felt an even greater sense of freedom after they invested the money in a manner that glorified God.

Others may rationalize that they don't give because God says we should give only cheerfully. Their thinking goes something like this: "God says I shouldn't give it away unless I can do so cheerfully, and so if I can't be cheerful, I should just keep it." It's disappointing when they use this as an excuse to hang on to their money. It certainly isn't the correct understanding of 2 Cor. 9:7, which reads, "Each man should give what he has decided in his heart to give, not reluctantly or under compulsion, for God loves a cheerful giver."

God tells us to give according to the purposes in our hearts; He doesn't tell us to "give cheerfully." It says that God *loves* those who give cheerfully. Why? Because the cheerful giver knows that the money isn't his or hers and holds it loosely. If we hold it loosely, we're happy to share it with someone in need, to support worthy causes, or simply to acknowledge that God decides where the money goes. The cheerfulness comes from the understanding, not from the giving itself.

Many of us haven't reached that place in life. We're too busy worrying about building our nest eggs, saving for college funds, and paying off the mortgage and credit cards. We want to hang on to what we have and what we earn so that we'll have enough for all of the things we need. But how much is enough? Is there a figure we'll settle for? When we reach that amount, will we give everything beyond that back to God? The question is silly. As we make more, we only want more. There isn't an end in sight. As long as we think of it as "ours," we'll never have enough. But you know what? There isn't an end in sight if it's God's either. When we give back what He's given us, it's supernaturally multiplied as it passes through the hands of His people.

Think of it this way. The $100 each of the members above received was actually his or her own money. A church doesn't earn money—it receives its money from members who donate it. When members donate funds to their churches, they're entrusting the leadership of the church to decide the best way to invest money in ministry. At Coast Hills, Bellesi and the missions committee decided to give it back to the members who volunteered on that Sunday. Those volunteers used their connections, talents, and creativity to multiply what they were given before giving the money to another worthy cause. Each time the money passed from hand to hand or individual to organization, God was able to multiply it for His purposes. Regardless of how much or how little members donated originally, the church combined it to make the $10,000 given to the 100 members who took their individual $100 and increased it, in some cases exponentially. Eventually, the media picked up the story, which led to other churches doing the same thing. If we read the stories on the Bellesi web site (<www.kingdomassign ment.com>), we see how God multiplied those original donated dollars beyond our earthly comprehension.

What could God do with what we give?

What could God do if we gave Him everything?

By giving Him everything, we're not suggesting you put the deed to your house in the collection plate on Sunday; we're saying we need to give up control and become stewards, not owners. How God would have us spend it, give it, or invest it is a prayerful matter between owner and steward.

Acknowledging that all we have is God's is an act of worship. It involves honoring God and submitting to His plan for our lives. When we give, we do so from allegiance and recognition of His lordship in our lives. We don't give to be cheerful—we give to be obedient. And God loves obedience. If $100 could change the world, how much could we change if we managed everything with that same sense of responsibility?

In this chapter we could have talked about the importance of investing for the future, tithing, saving for education and retirement, giving to ministry, and a lot of other topics about which Christian financial advisors write entire books. But we can figure those things out once we first figure out this truth—it's all His.

Charlie Chaplin figured it out. As he lay on his deathbed, a priest visited him and said, "May the Lord have mercy on your soul."

"Why not?" replied Chaplin. "After all, it belongs to Him."

If we ignored everything else in this book and did just one thing—offered our resources as if they were on loan from God— we wouldn't have to worry about our legacy. It would take care of itself. When it comes to the talents entrusted to us, God doesn't want our loose change—He wants us to have a loose grip.

Often we delude ourselves into believing things that aren't true, that we're deserving or that we've earned all we have. We need to change our thinking to realize how much we *don't* deserve and how we *haven't* earned what we have. We're indebted to God for everything, not only our money and our possessions but also our time and our talents. To believe anything else is to be deceived. The truth is, we owe it all to Him.

# 8

# Intentional
# INTEGRITY

Who told the first lie?

If we randomly ask people that question, many will guess Eve. If they don't answer Eve, they might say Adam, or sometimes they admit it's a toss-up between the two. But a review of Genesis shows that it wasn't either one of them. Of course, this famous first couple went on to tell the second and third lies, but they didn't tell the first lie. Satan holds that honor.

Adam was in the garden when God gave him specific instructions: "You are free to eat from any tree in the garden; but you must not eat from the tree of the knowledge of good and evil, for when you eat of it you will surely die" (Gen. 2:16-17).

In the next chapter we see that Eve is there too. We meet the serpent, who is described as being craftier "than any of the wild animals the Lord God had made" (3:1). "Crafty" is an interesting word. Try applying it to a dog. Doesn't work, does it? We don't describe an animal that lets its tongue hang out of a car window as crafty. How about a cat? We once had a pastor who believed that cats were evil, but have you ever met a cat that was crafty?

This serpent lives up to his biblical description. He approaches Eve and asks, "Did God really say, 'You must not eat from *any* tree in the garden'?" (3:1, emphasis added).

The serpent knew what God had commanded. Even if the serpent didn't hear it with his own ears, he knew it from observation. Adam and Eve had been helping themselves to the fruit from trees all over the garden, avoiding the one in the middle. Satan knew that if God's instruction was to "not eat from any tree," the first couple would have been really hungry. Obviously, God had told them to not eat from the tree *in the middle of the garden*, and Satan knew it.

## The First Lie

Part of the serpent's plan was to say just enough to get Eve to talk with him for a little while. He knew who he was, a snake in the grass or, in this case, maybe in a tree. He didn't mistake himself for a loyal dog or a clever cat; he knew he wasn't Eve's pet. He wanted to say just enough to break down the barriers and get Eve to talk with him. He did that by taking God's words and twisting them just a little, from one *specific* tree to *any* tree. He didn't start with an argument but with a question, but regardless of the phraseology, he misrepresented the truth—purposely.

He lied.

Eve should have smelled trouble. She wasn't used to talking to snakes. In fact, if she was like most of us, she probably tried to avoid snakes whether they talked or not. Her loyalty was with God. She loved Him, trusted Him, and didn't intend to eat from the tree in the middle of the garden because that's what God had commanded.

## The Second Lie

When the serpent seemed mixed up about the rules, Eve decided to set him straight and make the rules clear: "We may eat fruit from the trees in the garden, but God did say, 'You must not eat fruit from the tree that is in the middle of the garden, and you must not touch it, or you will die'" (Gen. 3:2-3).

In her zealousness to honor God, she misquoted Him; she stretched the truth. She warned the serpent that he had better not even *touch* the tree. It was just a little white lie, a slight embellishment of the truth, but it was OK, because it was for the serpent's own good. What she told him would protect him, not hurt him, and in that case it was OK to lie, right?

At this point, Satan had her, and he knew it. He told her that if she ate from the tree, her eyes would be open, and she would be like God, knowing good and evil.

We're not sure why Eve would want to know about evil. If she had hung out a few thousand years, she could have seen more evil than she ever cared to see on the six o'clock news. But chances are, it wasn't *knowing evil* that captivated her attention. It's likely she was intrigued with the idea of *being like God*.

She knew God, and she knew what He was capable of creating, because she saw it all around her. To become like someone she loved and admired was an enormous temptation. When Satan told her she could be like God, it created in her a longing—maybe even a jealousy—that never existed before. For the first time, she had doubts about what God had given her, and she wanted more.

Satan knew better than to hand her an apple and force her to eat. Instead, we can assume from the text that he encouraged her just to look at it: "The woman saw that the fruit of the tree was good for food and pleasing to the eye, and also desirable for gaining wisdom" (3:6).

She started by looking, then maybe put a finger out and "accidentally" brushed up next to the tree. Nothing happened when she touched it, and she fell victim to her own white lie. She forgot that *she* was the one who made up the part about not touching it, so she felt as if it were a confirmation. *Maybe it's OK after all,* she said to herself.

Maybe in her confusion, the rules seemed arbitrary. The fruit from the tree was oozing with juice; it was perfectly ripe—the colors, the smells, the intoxication of becoming like God. "She took some and ate it" (3:6).

## The Third Lie

While we can certainly blame Eve for being the first to eat the fruit, there was another lie being silently perpetuated. The last part of verse 6 tells us, "She also gave some to her husband, who was with her, and he ate it."

As this occurs—the conversation, the crafty serpent, the word-twisting, and the little white lie—Adam was there, and he didn't say a word! He knew the truth. He had also been around longer than Eve. God spoke directly to him, yet while these events unfolded, Adam never spoke up. He could have said, "It's not right—what you're saying isn't the truth," to either Satan or to Eve. Instead, he silently allowed both lies to go unchallenged. He condoned lying, which made him a liar by association.

## Truth, Lies, and the Evening News

The first lie wasn't an outlandish deception. Neither was the second or the third. Satan twisted God's words a little and asked a question. Eve was trying to protect herself and the serpent by embellishing God's original command. Adam didn't really lie; he was just quiet.

Thousands of years later, we use those excuses when we lie. We shade our words and meanings, we ask misleading questions in hopes of getting the answers we want, and we stand by in tacit agreement when we should speak out. We convince ourselves that we really aren't lying—it's all relative to the situation. But in honest examination, we can see that most of our gray areas really are black or white, muddled by an intention to mislead.

Need proof?

Watch the evening news, especially during a political campaign. The reports of the same event can look so different that we might not realize the two sources are talking about the same story. On one channel a statement is reported in context, the words and images as they happened. But subtle things, such as the phrases used by reporters in their lead-in or closing, can change the tone of the event. At the other extreme, with a little help from video and sound editing, crowds can look larger or more unruly than they were at the actual event. With words taken out of context and the banter between reporter and anchor, an innocuous event can seem sinister.

A memorable example of this happened during the 2004 Democratic primary elections in the United States. After a disappointing finish in the Iowa caucuses, Howard Dean tried to fire up supporters. He promised that his campaign would continue, and at the end of his passionate speech, he let out a primal scream that sounded something like "Yeeeeeearrrrhhhhh!" but written transcripts quoted it as "Yes!"

Since it took place on Martin Luther King Jr. Day, it was quickly dubbed the "I Have a Scream" speech and was shown on television hundreds of times over the next few days. Dean's speech was remixed with music for Internet downloads, was the butt of jokes for late-night talk-show hosts, and even became a reason to question his sanity.

It took a few days before some of the news organizations realized that Dean was holding a handheld microphone designed to filter out background noise. After interviewing those who attended in person and listening to the documentary tapes that had used a different type of microphone, it soon became apparent that the scream had been barely heard above the crowd. In context, it was nothing. Out of context, the "Dean scream" made Howard look ridiculous. It would be hard to find an employee of those media outlets who would call the original coverage a lie, yet it's obvious that the story wasn't reported with integrity.

Jennifer recalls a time when she had to make a decision about what was the truth. "I was supposed to pray for a friend, and I completely forgot that I had promised to do so. She came up to me and before I could say anything she thanked me for my prayers and said they really made a difference. She was gone before I could say that I hadn't prayed. I just stood there and thought, *I lied twice, the first time by promising to pray and not doing it, and the second by misleading her with my silence.*"

Maybe we're hesitant to say that twisting words, telling little white lies, and remaining silent deserve to be called "lying." How far can we stray from the truth before it becomes a lie? Where do we cross the line between truth and lie?

It's an interesting question and one we deal with daily. Is it right to tell my wife she looks good in a dress when she doesn't? Should I flatter my boss, even if what I say isn't true? Or how about the one many people use when the phone rings: "Say I'm not here."

When we discussed writing this chapter, we had a hard time finding a definition of truth that we thought our readers could agree on. While the Bible is absolute truth, how that truth is applied often varies, even among believers. For many the definition of truth is relative to some other standard, or based on personal experiences. But if "truth" is indefinable, then so is "lying." And if we're not telling the truth and we won't agree that we're lying, then what are we doing? How do we know how to act in the gray zone?

## The Question of Integrity

In light of our goal to leave a positive legacy, we decided the important question in a situation in which the truth may not seem obvious to us is *Am I acting with the utmost integrity?* For the serpent the answer was obviously no. Neither was Eve. Even though she had good intentions, she didn't act with integrity. She added her own rules to protect God's commands from being broken. In doing so, she let Satan believe that her words were exactly what God said. Meanwhile, Adam stood silently by. While many may say, "That wasn't lying, because he didn't say anything," there's no doubt he didn't act with integrity. While the political reporters in the Dean case will probably never come out and say they lied, it's likely they would agree the reporting lacked integrity.

There's no shortage of people who lack integrity. If you need proof, just look at politicians, because it seems a political scandal involving integrity is always going on. Don't they learn from past examples? Richard Nixon, the 37th president of the United States, was a commander in the Navy Reserves, served in the House and Senate, was vice-president, and was elected to two terms as president, though he served only a term and a half.

Bill Clinton was the 42nd president of the United States. He received a degree from Georgetown, was a Rhodes Scholar, and received his law degree at Yale. He served as attorney general and later as governor of Arkansas. According to the official White House web site, the United States enjoyed greater peace and economic well-being during his administration than at any other time in its history.

What unites these two men is not their lifetime achievements or even their successes; it's that they both lied during their tenure. Nixon not only lied to the American people about his involvement in the break-in of the Democratic offices at the Watergate Hotel, but he also encouraged his advisors to lie under oath. He may not have been a "crook" (his words), but he was certainly guilty of acting without integrity. His deceit led to both his resignation and to officials from his administration going to jail.

Years later, Clinton repeated the mistake when he dishonestly used his considerable verbal skills to twist his words and manipulate their meaning. His answers to questions in both press conferences and legal depositions definitely lacked integrity. His most famous example, "I did not have sexual relations with that woman" is a technically true statement—what he did didn't involve a bed, and there wasn't much relating going on. Later he said those famous words "It depends on what the meaning of 'is' is." Prior to his statement, who knew that we needed a definition of the word "is"?

Because of their respective lies, both of those accomplished, intelligent, and successful men were unable to fulfill their personal and political potential. Their choices kept them from being the superior leaders they could have been, and as a result, both will go down in the history books with an asterisk next to their names. They have forever tainted their legacies by their lack of integrity.

Our goal in selecting those two men isn't to throw political or even personal stones. We chose them because the consequences of their behavior on their legacies are so obvious. They're now famous for both their accomplishments and their lack of integrity.

But what about our own dishonesty? At one time or another, who among us hasn't been guilty of acting without integrity? Maybe we've taken supplies from the office or padded hours before billing a client who could afford to pay it. Have you fudged on expense reports or told the Girl Scout at the door that you had already bought cookies?

Each time we tell others that we'll pray for them and then don't, we lack integrity. We lack integrity when we borrow money from our kids' savings accounts, intending to pay it back but never doing so, or return an item to the store after we've used or worn it. We're as guilty as Adam when we stand by and allow others to tell lies or gossip without stopping them. Those indiscretions won't make headlines as Nixon's and Clinton's lies did, but our deceptions still have consequences on our personal legacies.

How do we make sure that we're acting with integrity?

We can do what Jesus did when Satan tried to tempt Him, as recorded in Matt. 4. Jesus answered each temptation of Satan with scripture, saying, "It is written" and quoted the truth. If acting with integrity and telling the truth is important to our legacy, meditating on verses that reinforce our beliefs can help us stand up against the temptation to twist our words, cover up our behavior, or stand silently by while others do the same. Living a life of intentional integrity is as simple as being deliberate not only about our words but also about their intended meaning.

Even if we're not important or successful enough for journalists to scrutinize our every move, we're important to the people who work with us, to our children, and to our spouses. They do scrutinize our every action, and if we act without integrity, we're giving them permission to do the same. Our lies or lack of integrity may never make headlines in the newspaper, but our integrity is important to those who depend on each of us as a friend, parent, or co-worker. If we lack integrity, the consequences directly affect each of them. Truth matters, and it matters most to those who love us.

# 9
## Conscious
# FIDELITY

I ran across the hot sand and got to the beach house just in time to hose off my feet before calling Craig. We had a 4:00 phone conference to discuss some issues related to this book. Since I was the one on vacation, I wanted to make sure I was prepared for the conversation. I turned on my computer and checked my notes. As the laptop came to life, I dialed, Craig answered, and after a few pleasantries we got into the planned conversation.

Unexpectedly, in the middle of the discussion Craig said, "Girl, if you were any cuter in that bathing suit you would knock me over!"

I was so surprised I hardly knew what to say. Being a little overweight (OK, a lot), I wasn't used to such compliments, but I had been trying to exercise more and I did have a nice tan from being at the beach all week. I wanted to say thanks, but it didn't feel right.

My second thought was *How could he see me?* Before I left town, Craig had me install instant messaging software that would help us communicate, but to my knowledge it didn't send pictures. *What else had he seen while I was sitting here adjusting my suit?*

Craig had occasionally complimented me in the past, but this was different. Craig is funny, and he often teases his friends. Yet this time he wasn't joking. His praise was so effusive that it confused me.

My next thoughts came in a rush.

*This is really inappropriate.* Craig was my Sunday School teacher before he was my friend and coauthor. His compliment and the way he said it was so over-the-top that the more I thought about it, the more uncomfortable I felt about what he said and how he had said it. I debated saying something, but I didn't want to hurt the relationship, and frankly, I was flattered.

*Should I just say thank you and let it go? Should I say something now or wait until I get back in town and do it in person? What would Craig's wife say if she had heard him? If so, why wasn't he worried about that? Should I tell my husband?* As the thoughts came faster and faster, I realized there was silence at the other end. Craig was waiting to see how I would respond. I inhaled slowly. I knew that I had to say something, but what I said could make all the difference in our working relationship, our friendship, and even our witness at church.

Craig broke the silence. "You should see Lydia! She's wearing a little lime green bikini with pink flowers on top. She looks so cute!"

Lydia is Craig's two-year-old daughter. His comment wasn't to me—he was talking to his preschooler! He wasn't making an inappropriate remark after all. He was admiring his daughter, who was waiting for Daddy to get off the phone so they could go to the pool. I was thankful I hadn't said anything.

## Inappropriate Images

Most of us have had inappropriate thoughts at one time or another. Temptations come when we misread others' cues, we attribute wrong motivations to them, or we stoke the passing sparks in our minds with lustful ideas and images.

In biblical times temptation was likely to occur person-to-person. Think of David and Bathsheba or Joseph and Potiphar's wife. But with modern technology, we don't need someone else to tempt us; we can tempt ourselves. Television is filled with people lusting after money, power, success, and of course, the opposite sex. Advertisers use scantily-clad models to sell products in magazines and on television. Even when surfing the Internet or using e-mail, we're accosted by adult web sites that try to entice us to check out inappropriate images. A recent study suggested that 74 percent of adult commercial sites display teaser porn pictures on their homepages in an effort to get us to click through.[1]

What's even worse is that our kids are also subject to those kinds of solicitations. Another study showed that 9 out of 10 kids aged 8-16 years have viewed porn online *by accident while doing homework.*[2] According to a study in the medical journal *Pediatrics,* the more sexual content teenagers watch on television, the earlier they become sexually active. Just like us, our kids are inundated, barraged, and enticed by sexual opportunities.

Temptation is everywhere, but what has made sexual temptation attractive to so many is that it's hidden. We can indulge in our fantasies without anyone knowing what we're doing. No one gains weight by viewing pornography, drives drunk by watching an adult movie, or gets lung cancer from a web site. We face those temptations in isolation, and we can give into them with a reasonable assurance that no one will ever know.

That's what happened to Craig's former coworker after they attended a trade show together. Because Craig made the hotel reservations, the charges were put on his card. When the executive checked in at the hotel he was supposed to use his personal credit card. After each returned home from the trade show, they were to submit their respective expense reports and be reimbursed by their employer.

After the trade show ended, Craig noticed extra charges on his card. He contacted the hotel and realized that the charges were incurred by the executive he traveled with. If his coworker had already turned it in on his personal expense account, Craig didn't want the company to have to pay twice, so he phoned the man's extension to ask about the situation.

When the executive learned what happened, he said he would be right down with his personal checkbook to reimburse Craig. Craig was surprised at the man's desire to take care of it immediately but figured he just wanted to do the right thing and make sure Craig wasn't carrying the additional charges on his personal account. As Craig studied the receipt more closely, however, he realized why the man was in such a hurry. The itemized receipt contained a $19.99 charge for an all-night pass of a triple-X feature. The executive was embarrassed to be caught doing something he didn't think would ever be discovered. Because he was on the road, he thought he could keep his activities separate from his life as a husband and father. The executive wrote Craig a check, picked up the receipt, and left without making eye contact.

Each time we choose something outside the bonds of our committed relationships, we take a step down a slippery slope. When we let our mind wander after watching a television commercial, when we turn on the afternoon soap operas, or when we use the Internet to look at inappropriate pictures, we're making a choice that has serious consequences to our relationships and ultimately to our legacy. Those seemingly innocuous choices add fuel to latent lusts and desires. Soon our appetites for those things increase, and then it's no longer occasional inappropriate thoughts. The thoughts become more frequent and wear us down until we lose our inhibitions and resolve, and eventually we act on them.

If we repeat an action often enough, eventually light will be shed on what we're doing in the dark. Like the executive above, we'll be caught. Someone will know. Under the right circumstances, a neighbor's satellite receiver can pick-up the pay-per-view movies we're renting in the privacy of our homes. It isn't likely, but it has to happen only once for us to be the joke of our neighborhoods. A trail of Internet surfing is stored on the hard drive, so the next time our spouses or employers choose to check our computer, they can see where we've been. The increased use of wireless technologies makes it easier than ever to track what our neighbors or coworkers are doing on their computers. Cell phones have been known to accidentally redial the last number dialed at the time we least want someone to listen to what we're doing.

Our current culture doesn't seem to care what people do in the privacy of their homes, and ultimately it shouldn't be someone finding out what you're doing that motivates you to stop, unless of course that person is your spouse or your child. If there's pornography in the house, whether in the closet, drawers, or computer, do you really believe that your children won't find it? If your spouse finds a secret stash of images, how can he or she refrain from comparing his or her body to those found in magazines? What does that do to his or her self-esteem?

Illicit behavior brings many consequences. People have lost their jobs for viewing pornography at work, and careers have been ruined by extramarital affairs. Perhaps the most devastating consequence is what it does to one's family. Viewing pornography and having an affair dilute the trust your spouse has placed in you, and that can ultimately lead to serious consequences for your family, including divorce.

Even if temptations aren't made public, God still knows our temptations and how we respond to them.

## Temptation Is an Opportunity to Choose Fidelity

It isn't the temptations that ultimately matter but what you do about them. "No temptation has seized you except what is common to man. And God is faithful; he will not let you be tempted beyond what you can bear. But when you are tempted, he will also provide a way out so that you can stand up under it" (1 Cor. 10:13). This verse contains two important points. The first is that temptations seize us. They don't fleetingly pass or accidentally wander in. They *seize* us, pull us in, and tighten their grip on us. The second half of the verse reminds us that regardless of the temptation or its stronghold, God gives us the ability to resist. We can make a choice to do what is right.

Sandi Patti is a five-time Grammy Award winner and a member of the Gospel Music Hall of Fame. She has received 39 Dove Awards, four Billboard Music Awards, and has sold more than 11 million albums. But her career took a detour several years ago when she admitted to having an adulterous affair that ultimately ended her marriage. Now remarried and fully restored in her church, she was quoted in an article for *Christianity Today* as saying, "I've learned that I am always a choice away from going down the wrong path."[3]

We couldn't have said it better ourselves, Sandi. It's a choice.

## Sin's Slippery Slope

Who would have thought that King David would have made the wrong choice? In the Book of Acts it says he was "a man after [God's] own heart" (13:22). Indeed, he did many courageous and spiritual things such as defeating the giant Goliath with nothing but a slingshot and writing much of the Book of Psalms. But even that warrior/artist fell into sexual temptation. For David, it began with a single image—as it does for many modern-day pornography viewers.

It started in the spring, a time when kings typically led their armies into battle, but David chose to send the armies off while he stayed home. One evening he couldn't sleep, so he decided to go for a walk on the roof of the palace. While up there, he caught a glimpse of a woman bathing. He could have turned away, but instead his eyes lingered, and he noticed how beautiful she was. That one image stuck with him, and he couldn't shake it. Eventually he called one of his servants and asked him to find out who she was. When the servant replied, "Isn't this Bathsheba, the daughter of Eliam and the wife of Uriah the Hittite?" (2 Sam. 11:3). David realized that he knew both her father and her husband. This king also knew that her husband was out of town fighting in the royal army.

David sent for her.

Under what ruse did he invite her back to the palace? We can only guess, but we know what happened next. After he slept with her, he sent her home. That might have been the end of the story. Maybe no one would have ever known of the affair—but later she sent word back to David that she was pregnant.

David knew this would look bad, since Uriah was away fighting. In the modern world, David might have paid for her to have an abortion, but in biblical times his choices were limited. He immediately tried to cover up his sin. He ordered Uriah back from the war and erroneously assumed that the returning soldier would sleep with his wife while home on leave, leaving no suspicions of paternity when it was discovered that Bathsheba was pregnant.

Uriah, however, refused to sleep with his wife in a comfortable bed when his fellow soldiers were sleeping on the ground. This confounded David's plan, so the king callously sent Uriah back to the front with secret orders to have the troops withdraw from him so he would be fatally struck. After Uriah was killed, David took Bathsheba as his wife.

Regardless of how we're sexually tempted, whether in person or on-line, yielding to the lures opens doors for us to lust after things we can't have. It creates scenarios in which we lower our resolve and sets up situations in which we can decide that it's all right, perhaps even necessary, to act. David began a quick descent off his moral throne by glancing at a naked woman and then committing adultery. In trying to conceal his adultery, he also became guilty of the murder of Uriah.

At any time during his descent, David could have made a different choice. He was one of the heroes of the Bible, yet an evening stroll and a wandering eye resulted in his being a murderer; his resolve left when his eye lingered. Most of us believe we would never go that far. That's the point—King David never thought he would go that far either.

Did the executive think that he was capable of adultery? Probably not. He thought he was just enjoying a few X-rated movies. But according to Jesus, he was an adulterer: "I tell you that anyone who looks at a woman lustfully has already committed adultery with her in his heart" (Matt. 5:28). A little pornography on the road may seem harmless, but to his wife, who could never live up to his fantasies, or to his two sons, who may someday model Dad's behavior, it's not so harmless.

## Why Is Fidelity Important?

The meaning of fidelity goes beyond whom we sleep with and how often; it has to do with being faithful, loyal, and devoted. Often we mistake fidelity as simply the opposite of infidelity. That is, if we're not having sex outside marriage, we think we're doing all right. But being loyal means concentrating our time, attention, and affections on our spouses, not on Internet images, trashy novels, or revealing television. Loyalty and devotion are crucial to long-term dating relationships and certainly to marriage. Seeking sources of fulfillment outside our commitments, whether in the words or arms of someone else, or even in our own image-inspired fantasies, creates a crack in the armor of our relationships. If that crack is compromised, it could be the end of the relationship.

Often Christians think they have some sort of immunity shield to resist the sexual temptations of the world. But that just isn't true. There are scores of overweight Christians who obviously don't possess special powers over tempting foods—so why should sex be any different? Do we need further proof that Christians aren't immune? Take a minute to recall the many successful religious leaders, musicians, and pastors who have fallen.

Furthermore, an affair doesn't have to be sexual. Only a small percentage of the population has serious sexual addictions, but almost all of us are susceptible to a little attention from someone outside our marriage. If you have a special bond with someone of the opposite sex at work or church that goes beyond working together, if you share conversations that your spouse isn't privy to, if you crave the attention of someone other than your spouse so that you feel better about yourself, your fidelity to your spouse may be in question. If you find yourself in such a situation, don't hesitate or linger as David did. Get away immediately. Then formulate a deliberate plan never to go back, regardless of how tempted you might be. The potential consequences are too great.

### Resisting Temptation

We all know how hard it is to stand up against temptation. Many of us have received what seems to be naive or trite advice on how to avoid temptation, recommendations such as prayer or Scripture memorization. Like us, you may have thought, *That's just too simplistic to be of much value.* But if you study Scripture, you'll see that those are the tools Jesus used when He faced temptation, and they can be powerful weapons in your fight.

Before He began his ministry, Jesus was led into the desert to be tempted. He fasted for 40 days and nights. Imagine the hunger and weakness He must have felt, because although He was God, His body was fully human. Satan knew that and came to Him at this low point, tempting Him by saying, "If you're really God, tell the stones to turn into food."

Jesus quoted Deut. 8:3: "It is written: 'Man does not live on bread alone, but on every word that comes from the mouth of God'" (Matt. 4:4). Twice more the pattern is repeated. Satan tempts Him, and Jesus fights back with scripture.

In *The Purpose-Driven Life*, pastor and author Rick Warren says that it's too difficult to change behavior by sheer willpower. Willing ourselves to act differently only creates stress, and eventually it becomes too hard, so we give up or give in to temptation. Instead, Warren suggests changing our attitudes. That's what Jesus did. He didn't use His godly powers to say, "I'm not hungry" or "I could if I wanted to." Instead, He fought Satan's temptations by focusing His thoughts away from how hungry He was and onto the truth He knew from Scripture.

Jesus also used prayer to keep from falling into temptation. He prayed constantly, sometimes leaving crowds so that He could go and pray alone.

He also taught others to pray against temptation. When the disciples asked Jesus to teach them to pray, He trained them by saying, "When you pray, say . . ." followed by the prayer we commonly refer to as the The Lord's Prayer. A key point of Jesus' teaching was for the disciples to learn how to pray not to be led into temptation (Luke 11:4). However, the disciples were a lot like us. No sooner did they hear it than they forgot it.

In the Garden of Gethsemane Jesus knew what was about to happen. In Luke 22:40 He specifically told the disciples to pray that they would not fall into temptation. He left them so He could pray alone. When He came back, He found them asleep. Once again, He told them to pray so that they would not fall into temptation. Just a short time passed, and as if on cue, each of the disciples was tempted to deny Jesus with perhaps the most notable example being Peter, who denied Him three times.

If the disciples had been able to resist temptation on their own, there would have been no point in Jesus telling them to pray. He didn't tell them to "steel your nerves," "strengthen your resolve," or "stay together as a group" to defeat the temptations that were coming. He told them to *pray*.

## Guard Yourself

Prayer can sometimes be used as a pseudospiritual way to give in to temptations. In the fallen world we live in, Christians who give in to temptation justify doing so with distorted claims that

Scripture supports the lifestyle or that God wants them to be happy. A pastor who was attracted to his secretary felt he needed to "come clean," so he invited her to lunch to confess his attraction, which until that moment she knew nothing about. A short time later, they began an affair that, once discovered, tore apart the church. Praying about the object of our lust may lead to an opportunity to fantasize more. If that's the case, it's advisable to seek counsel from a pastor or another mature Christian who can help guide us through "getting it right" with God first and *then* dealing with our temptations.

The easiest way to resist sexual temptation is to stay out of situations where it can occur. Each of us knows what our triggers are. Are you most likely to be tempted when you're alone, at work, or on a business trip? Avoid those temptation-sparkers as if your legacy depended on it. You could ask to have the television set removed from your hotel room or at least the pay-per-view disconnected before you check in. At home, carefully monitoring the television shows you watch and even what channels you allow into your home can protect you when you're flipping stations. You can use filters on your Internet connection or get software that will e-mail an accountability partner a list of every web site you visit. Be especially diligent when traveling alone with a member of the opposite sex, and while traveling, speak often and positively about family at home.

Billy Graham, easily the most well-known Christian evangelist of our time, realized very early in his ministry that sexual temptations tripped up too many ministers, so he took deliberate steps to do things differently. In his autobiography, *Just As I Am*, he describes the "Modesto Manifesto" he formed while traveling in Modesto, California, and which he has lived by ever since:

> We all knew of evangelists who had fallen into immorality while separated from their families by travel. We pledged among ourselves to avoid any situation that would have even the appearance of compromise or suspicion. From that day on, I did not travel, meet, or eat alone with a woman other than my wife. We determined that the Apostle Paul's mandate to the younger pastor Timothy would be ours as well: "Flee . . . youthful lusts" (2 Tim. 2:22, KJV).

Like Job, Graham was also intentional in avoiding temptation: "I made a covenant with my eyes not to look lustfully at a girl" (Job 31:1). We can do the same, but even better than making a covenant with ourselves is making a covenant with someone who will hold us accountable, someone with whom we can be honest and who will check up on us.

These things don't just happen—they require thought and pre-planning, but isn't it worth a few minutes of hassle to protect your relationships and your legacy? It will probably take less time to implement the steps we've discussed than it will to read this book. If your legacy is important enough to read about, it's important enough to guard. The best way to guard a marriage is for both partners to agree on rules and commit to follow them. We know marriages in which both partners are comfortable with their spouse having lunch with members of the opposite sex. In some of these relationships, there are rules that the one partner calls the other before the luncheon so that they hear about it from their spouse first. Other couples decide that it's never appropriate to meet someone of the opposite sex for lunch without a third party there. The important thing in these examples is that both spouses agree on the rules.

Barna Research[4] conducted a study that classified individuals concerning whether they had an active and personal spiritual life. According to the study, born-again Christians were equal to the non-born-again population in the incidence of divorce (35 percent), despite belief in the Bible and in biblical mandates that oppose divorce unless adultery is involved. The study says, "You can understand why atheists and agnostics might have a high rate of divorce, since they are less likely to believe in concepts such as sin, absolute moral truth, and judgment. Yet the survey found that the percentage of atheists and agnostics who have been married and divorced is 37 percent—very similar to the numbers for the 'born-again' population." Christians may not have an immunity shield, but God promises that we can protect ourselves and not give in to temptation when we're confronted with an opportunity.

The swimsuit incident between Craig and me took only a few seconds to resolve. I was particularly confused because Craig and I have taken deliberate steps to protect our respective marriages as well as our working relationship. For both of us, family comes first even if it means that we get behind on our writing goals. None of our correspondence is hidden; my husband or Craig's wife can look at our e-mails, eavesdrop on our phone conversations, or join our meetings. We also socialize as couples to keep the nonwriting spouses involved in what we're doing. They know where we're meeting and what we're working on at all times. We also believe that the best way to protect our marriages is to ensure that things are all right within our relationships. Protecting our marriages means not keeping secrets, resolving disagreements, and making sure our spouses feel loved and valued.

Most important, Craig and I are not naive about the possibility for temptations to occur. We're both conscious that even a chink in the armor of our marriages can be wedged open with outside temptation. We may think our little indulgences don't matter or that we have them under control, but sometimes even the simplest things, such as a lingering glance or an inappropriate thought, if indulged, can be a descent off our moral high chair.

If David, a man after God's own heart, could, couldn't we?

The good news, though, is the Good News. Jesus died for our sins—*all* our sins—whether thoughts or actual deeds.

In John 8 we read about teachers and Pharisees bringing to Jesus a woman caught in the act of adultery. They fully expected Him to endorse the punishment of the day—stoning. At first Jesus ignored their questions, but they persisted. Finally, He spoke the words we're so familiar with: "If any one of you is without sin, let him be the first to throw a stone at her" (John 8:7). No one came forward to condemn her. Jesus spoke directly to the woman: "'Then neither do I condemn you,' Jesus declared. 'Go now and leave your life of sin'" (John 8:11).

If fidelity is being faithful, loyal, and devoted, the teachers and Pharisees weren't concerned about fidelity; instead, they focused on the woman's *in*fidelity. By contrast, Jesus was the best example of fidelity. He was faithful to God, loyal to His friends, and devoted to His mission of saving us from our sins through His death. That kind of discipline—especially in the face of temptation—is rare, but with His help it's achievable.

# 10
## Dare
## to Be
# DISCIPLINED

Cal Ripken, affectionately referred to as "The Iron Man," played in a record 2,632 consecutive baseball games as a shortstop for the Baltimore Orioles. Prior to that amazing accomplishment, Ripken also set the record for consecutive innings played—8,243.

To set those records, Ripken did whatever was necessary, including playing while injured. In a 1985 game in Texas, he tripped over second base and sprained his ankle, but rather than take himself out of the game, he limped through the final six innings. When he hyperextended his elbow in a game against Minnesota, the injury caused him pain every time he swung and missed, but not when he connected. For the next six weeks he made sure that when he swung, he hit. Years later, he was quoted in the *Baltimore Sun* as saying, "I had some of my best days when I was hurting."[1]

Thomas Boswell of the *Washington Post* had this to say about him:

> Ripken conditions himself fanatically, year-round. He prepares himself each day to an extent most players can't comprehend. He builds his whole life around delivering his maximum performance for the team and to the public. He plays hurt. He plays tough. He busts himself to be a role model for your kid. In his worst year, he's still the shortstop you want out there EVERY DAY.[2]

Ripken didn't wake up whenever he felt like it, eat whatever he wanted, and watch a little television until it was time to go to the ballpark. He lived a disciplined and deliberate lifestyle. The choices he made allowed him to be in shape, healthy, and mentally ready to play through the long, hot days of summer, every summer, for years.

Maybe you're thinking, *Well, sure—he's a professional athlete and he's wealthy, so he probably has trainers to help him stay disciplined.* But discipline isn't something we can buy, and it isn't something we hope for. It's something we choose. How would our lives and legacies change if we chose to have that kind of discipline? We became aware of many areas in our own lives in which we lack the kind of intentional focus that made Ripken successful. Maybe you're the same.

## Making It a Habit

All of us have good habits, but many of us struggle with the bad ones. A bad habit doesn't have to be deliberate; sometimes it's the result of failing to do what we should. "I'll eat better and exercise more after the holidays," we tell ourselves, or "I'll get up early to pray tomorrow." But before we can accomplish those things, we're distracted, and we find ourselves doing the opposite of what we set out to do. And our habits don't affect only us. Good or bad, our habits also affect those around us.

If we really want to know what our most annoying habit is, all we have to do is ask those who live or work with us. They know if we're chronically late or always punctual. Our neighbors know what time we leave for work, how often we mow our lawns, and whether we clean up around the outside of our homes. But the people in our house know our habits the best. If you've ever heard the kids say, "Oh, Mom, not again!" whatever behavior preceded the comment will be a part of the legacy they talk about after you're long gone.

Maybe our habits aren't all that bad—just little things such as dropping towels onto the floor instead of hanging them up, or forgetting to put the cap back on the toothpaste. But even innocent activities, repeated often enough, have the potential to become dangerous to our relationships or even our health.

When does dropping a towel onto the floor move from "not a

big deal" to the thing that starts an argument with a spouse? Maybe smoking that first cigarette wasn't harmful, but somewhere along the way habitual smokers eventually may inhale packs that turn into cancer inside their bodies. Our spiritual habits determine the intimacy of our relationship with God. What happens when we cross the line from "I'll pray in the car on the way to work" to "I never pray anymore"? Even the simplest habit when repeated often enough becomes bigger than the act itself.

Lunch with a coworker of the opposite sex or watching an occasional questionable movie or television show may not mean much until we're being tempted on a regular basis. A lottery ticket here or there may not be a big deal until we start running short on grocery money or postponing other purchases to ensure we get the winning ticket. A drink with the guys doesn't seem like much until we start coming home late, missing dinner with the family, and causing our partner to question where we've been. Habits, such as smoking, drinking, not exercising, or not wearing seatbelts may be hazardous to our health, and the effects may last for generations, because those who view us as role models may imitate our behaviors.

Seldom do we honestly examine how our habits and even our habitual thinking processes affect our behavior. Instead, we just do what feels good or right at the time. Then, over time, it becomes a pattern. Unfortunately, that's the case with many bad habits—they make us feel better temporarily. Whether our bad habits include smoking, drinking, gambling, spending recklessly, speeding, or overeating, there's an initial rush of good feeling from those activities. That's why we repeat them. If we didn't get pleasure from them, they never would have become habits.

It's important to understand that every habit you have—good or bad—influences your legacy. Your repetitive practices tell people who you are—at work, at home, and in the community. Through your habits observers understand you. Do your habits enhance your life and legacy?

## Dare to Discipline

The best response to our bad habits is discipline—the kind Cal

Ripken had. Serious athletes develop discipline in every part of their lives in order to fulfill their competitive goals. They're deliberate about when and how much they eat, what types of exercises and strength-training they pursue, and even how much sleep they get. They consciously make those choices so that their bodies will be in the finest condition to perform at their best. Those choices become more than habits—they become a disciplined way of life.

Most athletes don't accidentally start eating healthfully one day and then in a few weeks it becomes a habit. On the contrary, they struggle with the same food temptations we all do. I'm sure many athletes would like an entire chocolate cake after a hard workout, but if they're serious about their goals, they pass those things up in favor of water and protein bars.

But that kind of discipline isn't unique to athletes; it's also observed in people who strive for excellence in other areas. For example, Kyle wanted to be a concert pianist. In order to meet his long-term goals, he had to practice, and that meant passing up many other extracurricular activities and social events while he was in high school. He played the piano for six hours a day during the week and for as long as eight to ten hours a day on weekends. Imagine a teenager sitting in one spot for so long!

Another example of disciplined living is provided by people we call "prayer warriors." Those people read and pray for hours a day. While many of us struggle simply to get in a few minutes with God, these saints wake up before the sun to spend hours alone with Him.

Musicians, dancers, athletes, and certain Christians have all demonstrated that living a disciplined life is possible.

If we're serious about what we leave behind, then we need to develop disciplines that will support our legacy, just as an athlete develops disciplines to support his or her performances. But the problem has always been how to take our bad habits or our sloppy ways and turn them into positive, intentional choices. After reading more than one or two of the thousands of books that try to get us to change our diets, start exercising, or stop bad habits, we can see that no matter how well-meaning the authors, a simple three-step plan won't make our bad habits go away. Those things aren't changed with cute, codified phrases. Change comes from a desire deep inside us. It takes an external power and a burning passion to stay the course when it gets tough, and it gets tough about 20 seconds after we've set the goal.

Ultimately, there's no quick fix to conquering bad habits and developing discipline. We hope that by understanding how repetitive behavior can become habits and how some habits are injurious and have long-term consequences, we can be inspired to make deliberate choices that result in a disciplined life. It's not about preaching or pointing fingers at bad habits but about being cognizant of our own habits and the lies we tell ourselves about them and choosing differently.

## You Choose

It's easy to read books by well-intentioned authors who write about the three steps we need to take to change. But if we're trying to change a bad habit into a positive discipline, a specific three-step program may not work for our specific individual habits, but *something* will. Don't give up after the first failure. Find out what does work. Be intentional about weeding out bad habits and cultivating a new discipline. It won't just happen. We must be deliberate and choose.

"Do you not know that in a race all the runners run, but only one gets the prize? Run in such a way as to get the prize" (1 Cor. 9:24). Think of yourself as an athlete competing against your former self for the gold-medal legacy you'll leave behind. But as athletes need help from a trainer or a coach, the God who saved you from your sins wants to be your trainer.

In Luke 11 Jesus taught the disciples to pray and specifically ask God to lead them away from temptation. We must ask Him to help. If we're sincerely trying to change, we should consider praying for negative consequences when we fail. We have to be really committed to change before we pray to God to ask Him to make things worse if we turn back, but what motivation that would be!

By becoming aware of our habits and examining them in the spotlight of our legacy, we can make deliberate decisions about whether our habits serve us and then consciously adjust them based on our understanding.

Did your parents have an irritating or unhealthy habit? Have you inherited it? More precisely, have you taken on their ugly habit as your own? You can choose differently. It may not be easy; it may take professional help or guidance to break an ingrained habit. You may have to humble yourself and ask for help. By not seeking help, you may be choosing to continue a bad habit that will become a part of your legacy.

Often we think that athletes are driven and disciplined because they hope to have fame and money. But even Cal Ripken, who has surely enjoyed the fruits of his discipline, realizes that it isn't the big things such as his incredible records that ultimately make his legacy great. He has been quoted as saying, "I've been asked this question a lot—'How do you want to be remembered?' And my response to that question has always been 'To be remembered at all is pretty special.'"

Writing this chapter forced both of us to ask ourselves "Are these the habits I want to be known for?" It made us deliberately choose which habits were good and which ones we weren't proud of. We can make a different choice about the bad habits we've carelessly created. In their places, we need to dare to develop the disciplines we desire.

# 11

# Give 'Em SOMETHING to Talk About!

Is there something you've always wanted to do? Sing in a band? Write a book? Skydive? Start your own company? Go back to school? What's that one thing that you privately think about doing but never quite get around to? Have you gone so far as to tell someone about your daydream?

There are risks involved in pursuing our dreams, perhaps money, fear, or danger. Maybe to do the one thing you dream of, you would have to give up life as you know it or risk failure in a world where you've known success. But if you're going to leave a legacy, would you rather leave one that showed you actually pursued your dreams or just talked about them?

Orville and Wilbur Wright dreamed of flying. At the time, what dream could have been more foolish, financially costly, or dangerous? But look at the legacy left to us by their pursuit of their dream. Without them, think how different our world would be.

Martin Luther King Jr. had a dream that all people would be treated equally. Everything he did was focused on making that dream a reality. How would things have been different if he hadn't followed his dream?

What did our great-grandfathers dream of? We probably don't know their dreams, but we might have evidence by their actions. Maybe they left the old country to start a new life in America, maybe built a successful business, or maybe dreamed of having a home that was radically different from the one they grew up in. The dreams that our grandparents have acted on have become part of the legacy we've inherited.

So you want to sing in a band? You may not be the next Bruce Springsteen, but unless you start singing, how will you know? Find a couple of musicians from church, work, or the neighborhood, and put together a weekend garage band. You might not tour the world, but you might land a gig playing at a company event or neighborhood picnic.

Have you always wanted to go back to school? Maybe you can't afford to quit your job and go full-time, but you could take an evening or online course. You might argue, "Yes, but it'll take seven years for me to finish." So what? In seven years you'll be seven years older; you might as well be seven years smarter!

Perhaps you've always wanted to get involved in foreign missions. If not you, who? If not now, when?

Your life will be richer from those experiences, and you'll meet extraordinary people along the way. Your kids or coworkers may not remember the "dreams you dreamed," but they'll talk about the ones you pursued.

"Can you believe Mom's book club is going skydiving?"

"Did you see Dad and all those old guys playing guitars and drums in the garage?"

"Can you believe she's going back to school after all these years?"

## The Courage to Pursue

But what if people laugh or scoff at your dreams? If your goals don't invite some doubt, they aren't big enough to be called dreams. If they were "for sures," you wouldn't need to fantasize about them. Part of pursuing a dream is doing it despite the people and circumstances that tell you it won't succeed. The way to avoid failure is to never try, and that's the biggest failure of all. Regardless of the outcome, when you attempt to reach lofty goals, you send a powerful message to those around you. We always tell coworkers that it's OK to take risks, and we teach our kids that it's good to try even when they don't succeed. Who among us hasn't told children they need to try something before they make up their minds about it? If this is true for them, then how can you justify not trying yourself? And what happens if you succeed? To some, that may be the most frightening part of trying. Successfully following your dreams could change your life!

God created us with unique gifts and talents, but He also created us with unique dreams. Leaving the kind of legacy we want to leave involves doing more than the ordinary—it means doing the extraordinary. The ordinary things of life, like brushing our teeth each morning, don't become a part of our legacy in the same way the extraordinary things, like inventing the first electric toothbrush, do. The legacy we leave is unique because each of us is unique.

Take a look at who you are. We're not referring to the person who crawls out of bed and heads off to work each weekday, but the person inside you who daydreams about the possibilities for the weekend, a new invention, or an absorbing passion. Find a way to help that person realize his or her dreams and goals, not for self-serving reasons but because setting that kind of example will leave a legacy that future generations will talk about. It will also show that it's acceptable to pursue God-given dreams.

Part of leaving a legacy is lighting a path for others to follow. What better path to light than one that shows others the way to their dreams?

## Help Others Dream

What if you don't have a burning passion? Maybe it's inside but you haven't found it yet. Think of Mother Teresa. It's probably fair to say that her dreams didn't involve going back to school or singing in a rock band. But when she saw poor and hungry children in India, her dream became one of caring for "the poorest of the poor." She began with 12 volunteers and opened a home for the dying in Calcutta, India. At the time of her death in 1997, there were more than 450 homes and thousands of workers worldwide. Because she acted on her dream, the world became aware not only of the plight of many children in India but also of the poor in our own communities. Mother Teresa gave us an example of what it means to be fully devoted to serving others even if it's uncomfortable. By all accounts, she led a deeply rewarding life and left a powerful legacy.

During his life, Sherwood Anderson was known for writing the book *Winesburg, Ohio*, but he left a legacy much larger than his book. In his short story "Mentoring," Jerry MacGregor tells of Anderson's willingness to help young writers. While he lived in Chicago, Anderson mentored a young writer almost daily for two years. Later he moved to New Orleans and helped a young poet write and polish his first novel. While Anderson may not be familiar to us, his legacy lived on in those two young writers, Ernest Hemingway and William Faulkner. Later, while living in California, he also spent time with Thomas Wolfe and John Steinbeck. MacGregor ended his story with the following observation: "Not only does it mirror my own experience, it also illustrates what I have found to be a fundamental pattern of human experience— that the greatest means of impacting the future is to build into another person's life."[1]

Maybe God hasn't called you to live in India or mentor yet-to-be-discovered writers. However, there's a place nearby that's crying out for volunteers; maybe it's a soup kitchen, a homeless shelter, or a tutoring program that needs you. By investing your time and talents in a community organization, you'll have the opportunity to instill hope in the hopeless. Even better than serving occasionally, you might consider dedicating yourself to an organization where you can make a difference and change things. You create memories that last not by investing in yourself (those memories are gone when you move, change jobs, or die) but by investing in those around you.

Think of it as depositing memories in the bank—except they can't be withdrawn. Regardless of your talents or skills, a charitable, religious, or community organization needs someone with your unique abilities. Just ask around to get more invitations to invest yourself than you will have time to invest.

When you're serving at a homeless shelter, take the next step and enlist family, friends, or coworkers to join you. Pick a holiday, or better yet, your birthday, and tell everyone you know that you'd like to celebrate your day by helping a specific charity or cause. Those who participate will share an unforgettable day with friends and family making memories and making dreams come true for someone else. Those who can't join you on that day but would still like to participate can be a part of it by making a small donation to the charity.

Think of how many people would talk about our birthdays if we all did that: the volunteers who celebrated with us, the donors who couldn't be there but contributed money in our honor, the staff of the organization who appreciates every volunteer and dollar that comes their way, and, of course, the public whom they serve. Although each of these people will have a special memory of our day, getting talked about isn't the reason to do it. If your motivation is for your own publicity, you'll never meet your goals. If you do it to serve others, your legacy will live on in the hope passed on to those you helped.

It's easy to think, *Yeah, that's a good idea, but I could never get my family or coworkers to do that.* It's true that not everyone will want to be involved, but then again, if we wanted to go bowling or to a Thai restaurant for lunch, there are those who would think those are bad ideas too.

No one has ever come back from a day of feeding the poor saying, "I wasted my day helping feed the hungry when I could have been home eating turkey and watching football!" People who volunteer their time talk about how it changes them, how great the experience was, and how they should do it more often. We can't let the naysayer's lack of vision destroy our legacies. People with meaningful legacies take risks.

## Take Risks

The greatest legacies left in the world of sports, politics, or even our Christian heritage are often the result of someone who took great personal risks.

Think of Jackie Robinson, who was ostracized by his own teammates and verbally threatened by fans, but he accomplished his dream of breaking the color barrier in baseball.

Think of Rosa Parks, who stood up on the bus by sitting down in the whites-only section.

Think of the founding fathers of the United States, who fought against England to create a new country with religious freedom.

Think of Abraham Lincoln, whose goal was to preserve the union at the cost of many lives, even his own.

Think of Martin Luther, who nailed his 95 theses to the Wittenburg, Germany, church door to encourage theological discussion and changed the prevailing theology.

If everything is simply status quo, there's nothing left to talk about. If you always choose the average or the ordinary, you'll leave a legacy like Chinese food—gone by mid-afternoon. People who leave the greatest legacies usually don't set out to create them. Instead, those kinds of legacies are created because they believe in something so much that they're willing to take great personal risks to help others.

There is no better example of this than Jesus Christ. No one shook things up more than He did. Religious leaders of His day believed He was the biggest threat to their faith in God, not that He was God in the flesh. Jesus said the Pharisees were greedy and wicked, and He called them vipers and hypocrites. Shaking things up wasn't just about calling them names. Jesus wanted them to change the focus from their strict interpretations of the laws to loving the creator of those laws—God.

A group of students from Kennesaw State University in Kennesaw, Georgia, saw an opportunity to shake things up. They started a Bible study in a Hooters restaurant. If you're not familiar with the restaurant, let's just say the name refers to more than the owl mascot. The students found by having a Bible study in such an unlikely location that they attracted seekers who weren't comfortable in a church.

Another example of shaking it up can be found on the Internet. Two youth pastors, Mike Foster and Craig Gross, have the number-one "Christian porn site" on the web—www.XXXchurch.com. Those who come to the site find Bible studies, educational information for parents to use when talking to teens about pornography, downloadable software filters, and accountability tools—all focused on the evil of pornography. While their methods are unconventional, they get more than 30,000 hits each week, and they post testimonials about how they've helped people break their porn addiction—an addiction Congress recently called worse than that of crack cocaine.

Some Christians fear creative demonstrations of their faith. They passively live their faithful lives and patiently wait for others to ask about their beliefs or to learn from their example. But Jesus wasn't a docile role model, and neither were the apostles. They stood up against the establishment for what they believed in and willingly suffered the consequences. If what we believe is important, why not shake things up a bit? We don't have to stand around shouting about it or hold Bible studies in adult-themed restaurants, but we can do it by seeking God's will for our lives. We can pursue our dreams and be open to the people we meet along the way. We can get active in our communities. We can support the things we believe in, even when it's hard, and even when no one else will. But most important, we should serve someone other than ourselves. That will certainly get them talking!

Jennifer recalls reading about a poll that said more people fear being forgotten than fear death. There's even a word for the fear for being forgotten—athazagoraphobia. If you want a legacy that lasts, if you want to be remembered, you must give people something to remember. Think of your life as a stone thrown in a pond; the ripples go out long after your stone sinks. Be the biggest, most inspiring rocks you can be.

Perhaps Mother Teresa's words give you encouragement to take that next step. She once said, "Yesterday is gone. Tomorrow has not yet come. We have only today. Let us begin."

# 12

# WORDS
## The Good, the Bad, and the Ugly

Kurt (name changed to protect the guilty) met a cute girl at a party. When she told him she went to a certain Christian college, he launched into a story about the school that involved a student who had slept with her professor and got pregnant.

The cute girl looked shocked as if she couldn't believe what he was saying, so Kurt continued with all the lurid details—including the girl's abortion. When he finished, the cute girl looked rather stunned for a moment. Then she quietly said, "I was that student."

What's the dumbest thing you've ever said?

Do you recognize any of these famous gaffes?

> "That man's ears make him look like a
> taxi-cab with both doors open."
> —*Howard Hughes on why he didn't want*
> *Clark Gable cast in a movie*

> "I think there is a world market for maybe five computers."
> —*Thomas Watson, chairman of IBM, 1943*

> "Smoking kills. If you're killed,
> you've lost a very important part of your life."
> —*Brooke Shields*

Kurt's example above was embarrassing, but he only made it worse with the words that followed. He was so surprised at the strange twist of events that, as he said, "At the time, all I could think to ask was 'Did I get the details right?'"

## Ugly Words

Even if the details are right—gossip is never right. If you've ever been the subject of gossip, you know the hurt it causes. If you've ever spread it, you're aware of the consequences. However, many are not familiar with the admonitions in the Bible against it. James 1:26 says, "If anyone considers himself religious and yet does not keep a tight rein on his tongue, he deceives himself and his religion is worthless." That's a strong statement.

We pay a huge price for gossiping. In addition to all the negative things that happen to the victim, there are also direct consequences to the gossiper. We lower ourselves in the eyes of others. Even if listeners seem to take a greater interest in us initially, it's usually just long enough to get the latest scoop. People believe we're untrustworthy, and we lose the opportunity to be a real friend or to have real friends. Our reputation is soiled, and more significantly, we undermine our credibility.

If you gossip, spread falsehoods, and betray trusts, how can someone believe you when you talk to him or her about your faith? Gossiping compromises your integrity and your witness. In 2 Tim. 2:16 we're reminded to "avoid godless chatter, because those who indulge in it will become more and more ungodly." That's a grave price to pay for boosting your own ego while sharing a few juicy tidbits.

During a Bible study, Suzanne asked if she could pray for Kristi and her husband, Brian. The other group members agreed. They suspected something was wrong because Kristi, usually a dependable member of the group, hadn't been there in a few weeks. So Suzanne, who was the kind of person who was always praying for other people's problems, prayed this prayer:

*Dear Lord,*

*I just want to lift Kristi and Brian up to you. Only you know how many women Brian has been sleeping with over the past few months, and how lonely Kristi has been.*

*Please forgive Kristi for getting a new boyfriend and bringing*

*him home to do drugs at her house. And I ask you to take special
care of her teenagers, who were traumatized when they got up in
the middle of the night and saw their mother smoking in the
house, because we know that's not the kind of example you want
set for those kids.*

*Lord, please bless the housekeeper who had to mop up the
bathroom floor after Kristi attempted to kill herself. Brian should
never have told her about his philandering while she was in such
a fragile state. Lord, only you know how they can afford the
housekeeper on Brian's salary, and now with him out of work,
even making mortgage payments will be difficult.*

*And most of all, we ask you to be with Kristi as she now re-
covers at Mental Acres. Help Brian know that we are here for
him so he doesn't have to lie and say she is visiting her mother,
because all we want to do is help. Amen.*

Everyone in the group knew that Brian was the youth pastor,
but they didn't know that he had been fired or the details behind
Kristi's lack of attendance. The biggest surprise was on Suzanne,
however—when she opened her eyes to see that Kristi had arrived in time to hear the prayer. With good Christian friends like
that, it's no wonder Kristi and Brian had problems!

OK—that really didn't happen, and it's an exaggerated example. But if we're around a group of Christians long enough, we
know that eventually someone will get around to fellowshipping
(that's Christian-ese for "the opportunity to gossip").

Gossip doesn't always start out maliciously. In fact, it often
starts out with the best intentions, especially with Christians who
believe in the need to intercede or pray for each other. In the beginning, our fictional gossiper, Suzanne, may have been truly concerned. But just as in her prayer, if we're not conscious of what
we're saying, our conversations can start with the right motives
but end by betraying confidences.

Crossing the line from care and concern to rumor-mongering
can be as simple as the difference between the words said and the
words left unsaid. "We need to pray for Kristi and Brian" works as
a prayer request. So does "We need to pray for some friends of
mine." Offering opinionated details about what we think Kristi

and Brian really need doesn't work. That kind of gossip does ir-
reparable harm. It ruins friendships, hurts relationships, and even
tears apart churches. We believe in the need to pray specifically
for things, events, and even people, but sometimes specificity
should remain in our private prayers.

Gossip isn't about the failings of the person we're talking about
—it's about our failings. We feel special, maybe even better about
ourselves when we have information that no one else has. Unfortunately, the only way for other people to know the juicy tidbits is to
tell them and break the confidence of the person who told us.

If we struggle with gossip, we should use conversation as an
opportunity to build someone up rather than take someone down.
Rather than talking about a pregnant and unmarried teenager, try
talking directly to the teenager and telling her how brave she is for
going through with the pregnancy. Instead of gossiping in our public prayers, we should ask to pray privately with the person. We'll
still have positive feelings but without the guilt. If we think gossiping will make us popular, we should instead try sincere encouragement. We all want to be around someone who makes us feel good.

Words are the most important tools we have to communicate
who we are, what we think, and how we feel. Ideally, all our words
are thoughtful, encouraging, and inspiring. But the reality is that
we can say things that are hurtful even when we have the best
intentions.

## Hurting and Healing Words

Though Nan is a writer, it wasn't her training in the writing
craft that taught her the enormous importance of words—it was
her mother.

Nan recalls visiting her dying mother in the hospital. She
looked so frail lying on the hard hospital pillows that when she
asked for a drink, Nan gladly picked up the Coke can and poured
it into the cup closest to her mother's bed. Then Nan held the cup
up so her mother could drink from it. Without even looking at her,
Nan's mother said through clenched teeth, "Not that one, stupid!"

Remember that old taunt "Sticks and stones may break my
bones, but words will never hurt me"? It may be a nice saying to

distract children from what's bothering them, but even very young children know that there just isn't any truth in that saying. Words can and do hurt. Whether someone intentionally delivers them to sting, like Nan's mother, or unintentionally drops them without realizing their effect, critical and demeaning words are like a cancer buried in the mind, that grows and spreads until one's whole being is sick.

Telling others they are stupid or worthless may not seem like a big deal, but if we're the kind of person who does that, it probably isn't an isolated event. Demeaning words are like a leaky pipe. It drips constantly until it gets fixed, and that drip is enough to ruin the wood cabinetry or carpet beneath the pipe.

Before her mother died, Nan knew that the only thing that could help her heal was the same thing that had been used to beat her down—words. Though her mother's words had always been cruel and rarely affectionate, Nan chose her words carefully. Though Nan couldn't recall the last time she heard affirming words from her mother, she leaned over the bed and whispered, "I love you."

For a moment, her mother's eyes cleared behind the morphine haze, and she smiled. Nan's mother didn't live long enough to discuss the effect of those words on her life, but they changed Nan and the way she thought of herself. "Reckless words pierce like a sword, but the tongue of the wise brings healing" (Prov. 12:18).

## Private Words

Sometimes the words we say in private are the words that have the most meaning. "I love you" or "I'm sorry—please forgive me" can be very powerful words. So can simpler sentiments, such as "You're very talented" or "I think you have a gift in this area." Whether we're talking to our children, our employees, or our friends, sometimes the simplest sentiments have a profound impact on the listener. Maybe you remember the encouraging words of a teacher or coach. Perhaps a mentor early in your career provided you with insight that has helped you succeed. Maybe it was a spouse saying, "I know how hard you work."

Just as these people have left a legacy of their words with you, you have the opportunity to pass on a positive legacy with your words. Just as you remember people, years from now the recipients of your encouraging words will remember your confidence in them.

You can get started on your legacy right now. You can change someone's day with your words. Look around—see the mother with the well-behaved child? Tell her. See the stressed-out executive? Remind him of his strengths. See the teen working the drive-thru window? Praise his attentive service. You can bet that each of them will repeat your compliment to someone else—"Do you know what he just said to me?" You just created an instant legacy.

God knows how important words are. "In the beginning was the Word, and the Word was with God, and the Word was God" (John 1:1). Linguists and anthropologists have spent centuries studying languages—their origins, evolutions, and differences from one another—yet God said that even before humanity was created, there was "the Word," and the Word was God. Communication and language are an inseparable part of the divine being. Your words are an inseparable part of your legacy. Are the words from your mouth the kind that you want others to remember forever?

## Prayer: Words to God

More important than the words you speak to others are the words you speak to God. Our prayers are verbal confirmations of exactly where we stand before our Creator. If our prayers consist only of immediate requests for tangible things—*O God, help me get out of this jam!* or *God, I need money to pay for this*—we're showing that we really believe God is an ATM who spits out answers to our requests. If our prayers are passionate pleas to do His will or to be more like Him, then our words are acknowledging that He is truly Lord of our lives.

The words we pray change not only us—they change others, as they see how our conversational communion transforms us from the inside out. The good, bad, or ugly words we leave will be our legacy.

Choose yours carefully, because the last word is often the word that lasts.

# part 3

## The Legacy You Inherited

*If you succumb to the temptation of using violence in the struggle, unborn generations will be the recipients of a long and desolate night of bitterness, and your chief legacy to the future will be an endless reign of meaningless chaos.*
—Martin Luther King Jr.

*This dress exacerbates the genetic betrayal that is my legacy.*
—Heather, in *Romy and Michele's High School Reunion* (1997)

*[Abel] died, but through his faith he still speaks.*
—Heb. 11:4, NRSV

*I have also seen children successfully surmounting the effects of an evil inheritance. That is due to purity being an inherent attribute of the soul.*
—Mohandas Gandhi

# 13
# A LEGACY
## of Prejudice

Some Americans have inherited a complicated legacy that sometimes includes an inability to get along with people of different races or nationalities. Native Americans called North America home until European settlers arrived and told them to move. Those settlers and their descendants then fought the British to keep control of the new land. When plantation owners needed men to work the fields, they "imported" people from Africa against their will. Those enslaved laborers were forced to work or risk beatings—or worse. Later, as immigrants sought opportunity in this new land, they settled in places like New York and Chicago. A racial pecking order slowly developed, with those on top often mistreating those below them.

We look back in horror at some of these evils, especially the evil of slavery. Others we acknowledge with misguided humor, with Polish or Italian jokes, for example. While our words may seem more sensitive than those of past generations, seeds of distrust have been planted, and when watered, they can still take root.

## Misunderstanding Motives

At Underground Atlanta, a popular tourist attraction in our downtown area, Craig once went into the men's restroom where he saw two muscular black men.

Craig turned around and was headed out the door when one of

them mumbled something. Craig turned to look at them and said, "I'm sorry—I didn't hear what you said."

The man repeated himself: "You can come in here. We ain't gonna mess with you."

It was at that moment that Craig realized they had made some assumptions about the situation. Craig was a skinny white guy from the suburbs. They thought he had come to use the facilities and, after seeing the two of them, thought better of it and left.

Craig quickly set the record straight, "I was just looking for a pay phone, and someone told me there was one in here. I didn't see one, so that's why I was leaving." Their look told him that they were as surprised by his statements as he had been by theirs.

We live in a very polite, politically correct society. We know the right words to say when the topic of racial or sexual prejudices comes up. We try not to offend others, and we're careful with our language. Yet we're still products of our history and upbringing. Craig and the two men at Underground Atlanta had a good laugh over the bathroom incident, because each person was thinking something different from what actually happened. But it was only by talking about the incident that they were all able to leave with an amusing, rather than a negative, memory.

## Inability to Trust

Unfortunately, we often don't take the time to talk about how we arrived at our different perceptions. In some cases, we're influenced by our upbringing and the opinions we heard while growing up. In other cases, we're prejudiced by the experiences of others. Too often, though, we simply inherit our beliefs rather than deliberately forming them. Regardless of how we develop them, we live in a time when our views about differences often separate us from others politically and socially.

For example, how many people believe justice was served in the O. J. Simpson trial? When white officers are caught on tape beating a black suspect, who is at fault? Studies show the answers to those questions are often racially divided.

When we hear that a child has been molested, do we immediately think that a homosexual must have done it? If there's a crime in the neighborhood, do we assume the skin color of the perpetrator before the police release the facts?

How we act toward people of a different skin color or nationality says much about our legacy. Do we trust people who are different from us? Do we give others the benefit of the doubt? Do we want to know people as individuals rather than labels? We can say the right words, but if our actions don't match our words we don't have integrity. If we believe all people are created equal, but there are certain ones we won't let into our homes, welcome into our churches, or work with at our child's school, our words ring false. Simply put, our actions reveal our prejudices even when our words don't.

When we look deep inside ourselves, do we believe that people of different nationalities or races are as honest as we are? Do we trust them as much as we trust someone who looks like us? Maybe we don't trust poor people because we think they steal, or rich people because we think they don't pay enough taxes. Maybe our biases are political—we don't trust Democrats or Republicans. Maybe it's small business owners or corporate executives we don't trust. Maybe our distrust is based on actual experiences with one of those groups. Or maybe it isn't. Maybe we simply inherited these prejudices.

Perhaps the worst legacy we've been left with is an inability to get along with people who are different from us. As we've become more sensitive to these issues over the years, we haven't overcome our biases; we've just gotten quieter and politer. Yet our actions still reveal our unspoken beliefs.

Trust is believing in what we don't understand or can't prove and acting on it anyway. Trust is faith coupled with action. Trusting people who are different teaches us how to trust God.

If we've inherited a legacy of distrust or prejudice, perhaps the most powerful legacy we can leave the next generation is the example of doing the right thing, regardless of the attitudes of those around us. Actions will inspire a greater trust than words will.

## William Wilberforce

When William Wilberforce was elected to the British Parliament at the age of 21, the only remarkable thing about him was his oratorical skills. He might have gone on to become a truly mediocre politician except for a conversation with a friend that changed his life. During a vacation from Parliament, a friend re-introduced Wilberforce to the Christianity he had known as a child. Over the next few years, his faith grew until it became the basis for his political decisions. Eventually he was known as one of the most conservative members of Parliament.

In 1787 Wilberforce was asked by a group of abolitionists to raise the issue in Parliament. He did, but his peers voted it down; however, during this process Wilberforce had his eyes opened to the evils of the system and became convinced that slavery was wrong. No longer just a man of words, he became a man of action. Wilberforce didn't let that initial defeat dissuade him. He introduced legislation again the following year. Again, it was defeated. Determined, Wilberforce continued to introduce the legislation each year *for 19 years.* Finally, in 1807 the British slave trade was abolished.

This wasn't enough for Wilberforce. For another 25 years he continued his campaign to end slavery, making his last impassioned speech when he was so ill that he could barely walk. After a long political struggle, the bill to abolish slavery in the British colonies passed its second reading in 1833.

Wilberforce died three days later. He had begun his political career with a reputation as merely a man of words, but he died a man of deep convictions who acted upon them every day for more than 40 years.

## The Legacies of the Atlanta Restaurateurs

For a more modern example, consider the legacies of two men who both owned restaurants in Atlanta in the 1960s, Lester Maddox and Ed Negri. Jennifer had an opportunity to interview both of them.

Maddox's restaurant, the Pickrick, became infamous in 1964 when the owner wielded an ax handle to chase away the Black men who tried to integrate it. Photos and stories from that day made him a hero to those who subscribed to his beliefs. But as forced integration became inevitable, rather than desegregate his restaurant, Maddox closed it for good. Instead, he opened a souvenir shop at Underground Atlanta, where he sold autographed ax handles. If he regretted his earlier actions, profiting from them wasn't the way to prove it.

Maddox was an amazing storyteller who lived a remarkable life, including a term as Georgia's governor. When his term ended, he served as lieutenant governor under Jimmy Carter.

As the last journalist to interview Maddox before he died, Jennifer was confused by his many contradictions. While governor, he put more Blacks into state jobs than all preceding Georgia governors combined. He integrated several state agencies and had close relationships with several of his Black employees. He made personal sacrifices fighting for the rights of Blacks in private situations; in fact, one of those incidents cost him his job when he had a young family and couldn't afford to be without a salary. Maddox claimed to be a follower of Jesus Christ and said all the things we would expect of a man who took his faith seriously and tried to live what he believed.

Yet his words couldn't blot from his legacy the stain of his public behavior. Was he a racist or merely a segregationist? A misguided Christian or a spiritual pretender? Jennifer left more confused than enlightened about his character; but one thing she's sure of is that his action on that day in 1964 did more to affect his legacy than did all his spiritual talk. To this day, politicians and journalists use his infamy as the ultimate insult by saying an opponent is "just like Lester Maddox." Regardless of Maddox's intentions or motivations or what actually occurred that day at the restaurant, Jennifer knows that the man she interviewed would not have wanted his legacy to be used as a political insult. Unfortunately, that's the public legacy he left.

Contrast Maddox's legacy with the legacy of another restaurant owner. Ed Negri would have us believe he was the Forrest Gump of the restaurant business. For nearly half a century his family owned and operated Herren's Restaurant on Luckie Street, the hub of Atlanta's political, social, and business web, before it closed in 1987. Like the fictional movie character who had accidental experiences with some of America's most important people, Ed also rubbed shoulders with Atlanta's and the nation's elite.

At Herren's, the home of the original power lunch, politicians, journalists, and businessmen dined and closed deals over cinnamon rolls and Shrimp Arnoud. People such as actors Caesar Romero and Bela Lugosi and golf great Bobby Jones ate at Herren's, as did a young billboard salesman named Ted Turner. But even his famous customers couldn't help Negri avoid the integration issue.

When I interviewed him, he recalled details of the events that preceded the desegregation of Atlanta's restaurants. He remembered reluctantly attending a meeting of restaurant owners in which the owner of a local mall talked about the police beatings that had occurred earlier that year in Birmingham and of the "blood running in the streets." Negri remembers the speaker saying, "Summer is coming, and we've got Atlanta University here with thousands of Black students. They aren't going to have anything to do. You've got to know there's a possibility that some of that could happen over here. You guys ought to think about that now, before it happens, and decide what you're going to do."

This was a difficult decision for Negri. Herren's faced increasing competition from private dining facilities that didn't have the same pressure to integrate. If he chose to open his restaurant to Blacks, he knew his white customers would probably choose to eat at private clubs rather than at his restaurant. Despite his concerns, he continued to attend meetings.

He recalls one meeting at the Riviera Motel, where a vote was taken on the integration issue. The speaker turned to the man on his right, and that owner said, "Let's do it." The vote went around the table and ended with Negri's vote. It was unanimous.

"If he had started with me, I don't know what I would have said," admitted Negri.

At a final meeting held at Lenox Square shopping mall, the owners decided to voluntarily desegregate their restaurants. At the conclusion, Negri reminded the attendees that a reporter would be waiting for them. Someone suggested the need for a spokesperson. "When you've been dead 50 years in your coffin, it won't be as quiet as it was then," remembered Negri, who eventually volunteered. "It didn't dawn on me that I was committing suicide."

Negri asked what he should tell the reporter.

"Tell him, 'No comment,'" came the reply.

"You can tell that yourself!" snapped Negri, who told the reporter of the restaurant owners' unanimous plans to voluntarily desegregate. "I was quoted. Several guys helped me, but it was agreed that they wouldn't be identified. As far as Atlanta was concerned, I was the first and the only one. I didn't do it because I was a hero. I thought, 'I got 50 guys back there who were all going to do it.' And they all did, but they wouldn't say so."

"Negri was the only restaurant owner who would comment on the results," said Don Rooney, curator of urban history at the Atlanta History Center. "He publicly expressed his views that all should be able to eat where they chose, and as a result his restaurant was picketed by whites."

When Ed told Herren's managers of the decision, his mother was at the meeting. "I told them what had been going on, and I said the decision had been made, and today we are going to serve our first Black customer."

Recalling that moment, Negri's voice cracks. "My mama said, 'What took you so long?'"

Next, he informed the staff saying, "You are expected to give them the same lousy service you've been giving everybody. If you don't want to do it, nothing will be said about it. This is my decision, not yours. You can leave if you want." No one left.

A few days later, a Black doctor with his wife and mother were the first to integrate the restaurant and were seated in the alcove. "We sat at the front table in that dining area so we could be sure nothing happened," said Negri's wife, Jane. "We were there, and everything went as smooth as silk."

"I figured I was the bomb-catcher. If somebody threw something through the window, I wanted to be the one to catch it," said Negri. It was a courageous decision, but one made with fear for the unknown. In the same year as Martin Luther King Jr.'s "I Have a Dream" speech, Negri lost loyal customers, endured picketing by the Ku Klux Klan, and lost $20,000 worth of business—a substantial portion of the restaurant's annual income.

Jennifer spent an entire day with Ed and his wife, Jane, and not once did she hear them talk about their faith, their church, or their religious beliefs. To this day, she doesn't know where they stand on those issues, but she does know that Negri's legacy will forever shine as an example of actions that speak louder than words.

## Actions for the Next Generation

The Negri legacy doesn't stop there.

The difficulties that Negri and his family faced at Herren's because of his decision only further cemented his resolve. Negri went out of his way to make everyone who dined or worked at his restaurant feel like part of the family. Several employees worked there for as long as 30 years. The place felt less like work than it did an extended family. And just like a family, Negri left a legacy among his employees that went on for generations.

Blanche Matthews, affectionately called the "white-haired grandma," worked as a Herren's waitress for 33 years until the day she died at age 74. Blanche lived with her daughter, Connie McTaggart, and Connie's husband in a beautiful home in the suburbs, but each day Blanche took the bus downtown to work at Herren's restaurant. She did it because she loved the people there.

Over the years, Blanche saved a little money. Before she died, she asked Connie to use it to take care of Johnny, a Black busboy who worked with her at Herren's. For years after her mother's death, Connie honored Blanche's request by mailing a check to Johnny and his family each Christmas.

This is just one example of how Negri's legacy continued in ways Ed didn't see or expect. He touched more than just his employees; he touched the lives of his customers, as well as his employees' families, long after the restaurant closed.

## Choose to Act Differently

We've integrated our schools and our restaurants, but have we successfully integrated our spiritual communities? Perhaps the most segregated place in the United States is a church on Sunday morning. Despite our commonalities, the church remains one of the most racially separated institutions in our country.

If we've become heir to a legacy of prejudice and distrust, or if we realize that our words and actions may be leaving such a legacy for future generations, we can start a change today. But we can't change a legacy with good intentions or well-motivated words — only our actions can leave the kind of legacy modeled by Wilberforce or Negri. To overcome the hate, distrust, and prejudice we see around us, we must establish one-on-one relationships that will help us grow into a nation of people who aren't prejudiced. Can we commit to build that relationship with someone different from us?

To overcome prejudice, we must develop trust. And trust is developed through integrity. If our words say one thing and our actions something else, we don't build trust. We need to reexamine our family's legacy of distrust one relationship at a time. We need to get to know someone of a different race, not just through our words but through our actions. If we each take steps to break down the barriers of suspicion and mistrust, not only will we change our legacy for future generations, but we'll change the legacy left for another family.

Just as a son adopts his dad's favorite team and later roots for it on his own, many of us unconsciously carry forward the prejudices we learned as children. To change that legacy, we must learn to trust those who are different, forgive those who have wronged us, and make sure our actions live up to our words.

Lester Maddox's actions will be remembered long after his words are forgotten. So will Ed Negri's.

# 14

# Unhealthy LEGACIES

Do you remember the last television news report or special program you saw about sick and dying children?

Craig doesn't, because he refuses to watch such news programs. "My wife laughs at me, but I refuse to do it," says Craig. "My perspective is that I can't help them, and it is too depressing to watch. It tears me up."

There are some things we can't control. One of those is our genetic inheritance. Perhaps we're prone to heart disease, tooth decay, high blood pressure, or elevated cholesterol levels. We can do things to improve our health, but we can't change a legacy that includes a propensity towards heart attack, stroke, or cancer.

At a certain point, we have to deal with the legacies we've inherited regarding our health, and that may mean dealing with disease. Even if we're healthy, we probably know someone whose life has been affected by a chronic illness or chronic health problems. If that someone is a spouse, not only will we have to deal with the illness in this generation, but if the disease has a genetic component, we'll have to deal with the possibility of our children inheriting it.

Maybe you're angry about your health heritage. You didn't deserve it, you didn't choose it, and you certainly didn't create it. It was the gene cocktail you inherited from your parents, and there's little you can do about it. But in his letter to the Romans, Paul says you should be happy about it.

He writes, "We also rejoice in our sufferings, because we know that suffering produces perseverance; perseverance, character; and character, hope" (Rom. 5:3-4). He makes similar statements elsewhere: "Rejoice in the Lord always. I will say it again: Rejoice!" (Phil. 4:4); and "Give thanks in all circumstances, for this is God's will for you in Christ Jesus" (1 Thess. 5:18).

While scholars disagree about the particular circumstances that caused Paul to write these words, they generally agree that his words are true and applicable regardless of personal situations. But when you're dealing with difficult issues such as chronic health problems, it's not easy to apply Paul's message.

Jim was facing some tough personal struggles. When he read Paul's words, he got mad. How could Paul tell us to be happy during suffering?

"I hated Paul," says Jim. "He says to rejoice in our suffering, but even Jesus didn't rejoice in His suffering. Instead, He prayed that if it were God's will, His cup would be taken away and His suffering end. He prayed that twice! Was Jesus rejoicing then?"

When Jim sought advice from his Christian friends about his frustrations, they weren't understanding. "When I talked to people about the fact that I hated Paul because he wanted me to do something that even Jesus didn't do, my friends said that I had a problem with Jesus, but I told them it wasn't Jesus—it was Paul I had a problem with. Jesus I understood."

Jim struggled through a difficult year, but because of his personal suffering, he eventually learned something that changed his mind about Paul. "I learned that Jesus was the only person whose suffering took Him *away* from God. All suffering since then brings us *closer* to God if we let it; that's why Paul said to rejoice in our suffering— because it brings us closer to God." Only by going through his own suffering could Jim finally understand Paul's message.

Does your illness or suffering bring you closer to God?

It can.

Ill health can be an opportunity to take control of the things we can affect, such as eating properly and getting sufficient sleep. It can also be an opportunity to yield control of things we can't have power over. Illness can become a metaphor for life. Sickness can teach us that we do have choices to make that affect our health. There are also many afflictions that we can't manage, that we don't understand, and that seemingly attack us. But regardless of whether or not we're in control of these things, we do have hope. That hope is in the Lord, who controls everything.

## Attitude

If you have high blood pressure, you may manage it by eating right, exercising, taking medication, and avoiding stress, but you can't do anything to prevent the propensity for high blood pressure from being passed on to your kids. The sickly genes you inherited will go on for generations, but so will a healthful lifestyle that prevents those genes from realizing their full potential. Along with those genes you can pass on an attitude of acceptance that acknowledges the potential for a blessing, not just a burden.

Jennifer is an insulin-dependent diabetic. She wears a pump that controls her medication. Every three days she must take the plastic cannula and tubing out of her stomach, refill a syringe with insulin, reassemble the pieces, and reinsert a fresh set.

When her son was three years old, he was watching her do this and then picked up a vial of insulin and tried to push it into his belly button, "Look, mommy—I pump," he said. Another time as he was playing with some of her supplies, she stopped him, which, of course, frustrated him. "I want to be a diabetic when I grow up!" he said and stomped out of the room.

"While my immediate reaction was 'No, you don't,'" said Jennifer, "later it occurred to me that he didn't see any stigma in my health problems, and that made me happy. But it was only while writing this book that I realized it was a legacy I had passed on to him, one I had received from my parents. Even though I was only eight years old when I was diagnosed, my parents made sure my diabetes didn't stop me from doing anything other kids did or from completing any goal I made for myself. I grew up knowing my parents didn't see my diabetes as an excuse, so neither did I. Now I can see that my son has inherited the same attitude."

Craig also lives with a long-term illness in his intestinal tract. Separately, we have each chosen to make the most of each day. We have both, independently, decided that we would not allow our circumstances to take away from the quality of our lives. In fact, our diseases have motivated us to appreciate the days when we feel healthy and to live our lives to the fullest.

In the movie *Dead Poets Society*, Robin Williams plays the role of a teacher who feels it's important to stretch his students' minds and to encourage them to live to the fullest. His motto is *Carpe Diem,* or "seize the day." With a chronic illness, this attitude becomes even more important as we have a heightened sensitivity to the fact that all of us have days that are numbered and that good days are something to be appreciated. No one knows the value of a day more than someone who's dying.

New medical research has shown that patients who display a positive attitude and laugh frequently also heal faster, have fewer heart attacks, and live longer. Understanding the importance of each day we're given and seizing that day with a positive attitude makes life not only happier but healthier as well.

## Who's in Control?

If you've inherited an unhealthy legacy, you can't control the fact that you received it or that you may pass it on to future generations. It may feel as if everything is out of control, but that's not true. Learning how you can gain control over your body may actually help improve your attitude. Improving your attitude improves your health.

To find other areas you can control, you can learn as much as possible about your personal health situation. Not going to the doctor because of a fear of cancer is the most harmful thing you can do. If it's cancer, it will only get worse without treatment. Not dealing with reality doesn't make an illness any less real. The stress of worrying can also be physically harmful. Going to the doctor for a proper diagnosis is the first step in understanding what, if anything, is wrong. Discussing treatment and disease management options with a doctor, reading books, and studying information on the Internet can help you understand what you can expect and what things you can control.

Paul writes "Do you not know that your body is a temple of the Holy Spirit, who is in you, whom you have received from God? You are not your own; you were bought at a price. Therefore honor

God with your body" (1 Cor. 6:19-20). We don't honor God by failing to take care of ourselves.

## In the Eye of the Beholder

Many people believe that part of taking care of oneself includes trying to be thin and beautiful, and they have resorted to drastic measures to reverse the genetics they've inherited. Jocelyn Wildenstein is the queen of bad plastic surgery. Her pictures have been in magazines and on television. She's the billionaire socialite who succeeded in getting her face to resemble a feline. Dubbed "Cat Woman" by the media, this woman has less in common with Halle Berry's movie role than she does with Michael Jackson's real life.

Looking in the mirror, what do you see? Are you happy with your appearance? For most of us, there's a lot we would like to change. Maybe you don't like your nose, your teeth, your receding hairline, or you think you're too fat. How much of this is real, and how much of it is media-inspired? Do billboards, television, and Photoshop-perfected images in magazines play a part in the demand for beauty? If we weren't exposed to reality shows that glamorized plastic surgery, would there be a reduced demand for people to surgically alter their appearance?

The question today might be—Is our dissatisfaction with our appearance real or advertiser-inspired? For example, consider the recent explosion in teeth-whitening products. A few years ago this product line didn't even exist. The only people who thought about the color of their teeth were professional actors and models. These days it's expected that if your teeth aren't glistening white, you had better keep your mouth shut or use expensive chemicals or cleaners to remove the stains and lighten the look. According to the advertisers who sell these products, if you don't, you may not get a date, or even a kiss from your spouse.

As advertisers and the media send the message that we need to change who we are, we're unconsciously accepting their suggestions as the definition of true beauty. As a result, our dissatisfaction with our own appearance only grows as we realize we can't meet that supermodel standard of perfection.

We see the results in the number of teenage girls suffering from anorexia and bulimia. Parents of pre-teen and teen girls are especially concerned about this trend as their daughters try to avoid the normal weight gain associated with growing bodies.

Children and teens aren't the only ones who are susceptible. Recently a friend expressed concern over his wife's desire to have plastic surgery. He blames the desire on friends from her tennis team who have "had a little work done," yet he fails to see how his jokes about saving enough money to "buy" his next girlfriend's looks affect his current wife's opinion of herself. That she's already thin and beautiful seems to be beside the point. Both of them have bought into the idea that it takes surgery to conform to an outside standard of beauty.

We can blame our parents, we can blame the media, but truthfully, maybe we need to blame God for whatever it is that we don't like about our looks. After all, He created us in His image. But then, look at Eccles. 3:11—"He has made everything beautiful in its time." By His standards, his work is beautiful. After He finished creating human beings, He said, "It is good." The Psalms say we should praise God because His works are wonderful and we're wonderfully made. So if we don't see beauty where God does, what's wrong with us?

Could it be that it's our definition of beauty that's messed up? Consider this verse from Proverbs: "Charm is deceptive, and beauty is fleeting; but a woman who fears the LORD is to be praised" (Prov. 31:30). Appearance is fleeting regardless of how many times it's corrected through surgery. Real beauty is found in the fact that God made us to be more than just how we look. If we choose to focus on Him instead of us, we will have made a choice that is praiseworthy, regardless of our physical inheritance.

Could we have inherited precisely what God intended? God says, "Before I formed you in the womb I knew you, before you were born I set you apart" (Jer. 1:5). God paid attention to the details; He was the one who formed us in our mother's womb. He made the decisions about our hereditary bodies. If a mother thinks her baby is beautiful, imagine how beautiful the God who formed us in her womb must think we are.

We have very little control over the body we inherited, and while we can try to improve on our looks, our education, and our talents, there's still much that we can't control. How you choose to react to your reflection in the mirror, how you define your beauty, and your relationship to the God who formed you and loves you becomes the legacy you pass on to those you love.

## Learn to be Content

Most of us wish we had better looks, more money, and a healthier body—but one of the most important biblical concepts is the idea of being content no matter where we are, regardless of what we have. The same Paul who told us to rejoice in our sufferings told us in his letter to the Philippians that he is content in every situation. (Yeah, right—sounds like something else Jim should get angry at Paul about.) But biblical scholars believe that Paul may have had some kind of long-term illness that was his "thorn in the flesh," so he knew what he was talking about.

How can we be content in the circumstances we're facing? First, make a vow not to waste time worrying about the things we don't have. Even Donald Trump and Oprah Winfrey want more, supermodels still feel ugly in the morning, and muscular athletes feel compelled to take steroids. There will always be people who have more than we do, but there will also be people who have less. We must make up our minds not to be obsessed about it anymore.

Second, we can thank God for the things He has already given us. It may not be much, or it may be a lot, and we just don't see how much we really have. We can ask Him to reveal all the blessings in our lives and try to write them down so we'll remember them when we don't feel so thankful. When Pamela was receiving chemotherapy for her cancer, her hair fell out. Later she said, "Now I'm thankful for eyelashes and nose hairs." Gaye suffers from Lupus. Sometimes she breaks out in a rash, and yet she says, "I'm thankful the rash is under my clothes."

Third, while thanking God for the good things in our lives such as family, friends, an afternoon without a headache, or whatever it is that we're thankful for, we're putting things into the right perspective. We're making God the center of our lives. Paul writes, "Godliness with contentment is great gain. For we brought nothing into the world, and we can take nothing out of it" (1 Tim. 6:6-7). Thank God, because it really is from Him that all our blessings flow.

Finally, one of the best ways to be content is to serve others. Even if you're too ill to leave the house, you can still make an encouraging phone call, pray for others, and write a note or e-mail. Doing for others will help you feel better about yourself. Unlike your health, self-esteem is earned. One of the best ways to feel good about yourself is to serve someone else, but to see the other person's need, you must get your eyes off yourself.

LeAnne knows what can happen when one focuses only on oneself. In our Sunday Bible class, she told of her trip the previous week to visit her parents. Her husband and four children, along with their dogs, were in the car with her. As she was driving, she noticed something on her shoe and took her eyes off the road for a second to remove it, but in doing so she crossed the middle line. When she looked up, she corrected and was able to get back on the right side of the road, but a car coming in the other direction had moved to avoid a collision with her and wasn't so lucky.

LeAnne watched in her mirror as the car flipped over three times before coming to rest on the side of the road. LeAnne knew everyone in her own car was all right, but she feared the driver in the other car might be dead, because the damage was so devastating. They pulled over and found out that, amazingly, everyone in the other car was all right. During prayer time LeAnne remarked, "Just taking your eyes off the road for a second can be very dangerous."

Isn't that like our relationship with God? Taking our eyes off Him for a second to look at ourselves may not cause us any immediate harm, but it could cause those on the same road with us to crash. Our actions and our attitudes about ourselves may not seem like a big deal, but they can and do impact the people around us, sometimes without our even realizing it. Next time you look in the mirror, think about leaving a rich inheritance. Keeping your eyes on God and not on yourself is the richest treasure you can leave.

# 15
## Spiritual LEGACIES

In addition to receiving a legacy from his parents, Craig received a spiritual inheritance from a youth pastor, a minister of music, and a very boring Bible teacher he called Snoozer. Craig jokes that he started going to church nine months before he was born. Church life was important to both his parents, and he can't remember a time he wasn't involved in church activities.

From his middle school years he remembers a youth pastor who had a great zeal for the Lord. That man of God taught Craig to love the Lord with passion. Craig's music minister taught him to appreciate God's gift of music and the endless ways of praising God with it, a lesson that has stayed with him. Both of those godly men encouraged Craig to have a daily, personal, and intimate relationship with Jesus.

And Snoozer? Craig received a spiritual inheritance from him too.

"We had a guest-speaker from our denomination coming, and I wanted to invite a friend to church, but I didn't get around to asking him, so it was just me and my family. I listened to Snoozer for what seemed like a week, though in actuality it was probably only a couple of hours. I can't remember a thing he said, but I do remember how boring he was, and the way he talked about the Bible made me want to leave. I remember thinking how glad I was that I hadn't invited my friend."

Many of us have had similar experiences with a guest speaker, or worse, the pastor of the church we grew up in. The limitations of the person delivering the message destroyed our hope of getting meaning out of the content. But even if the spiritual legacy we received from a church or minister was a "boring" one, that legacy could still affect us positively.

Craig may not have gotten much from the speaker that night, but the guest's poor delivery affected Craig's spiritual life forever. "I made a commitment that night that I would never talk about the gospel in a way that seemed boring. I vowed always to share that the Word of God is alive and exciting, something to be celebrated. The Bible is full of unbelievably exciting things." For the past 17 years as a Bible teacher, Craig has had the opportunity to teach alongside other Bible teachers, and his consistent message has always been "Make it fun."

Jennifer inherited her spiritual legacy from both family and friends. "I was in a family that had two kinds of Catholics: good Catholics (those who went to church) and bad Catholics (those who didn't). We were good Catholics, so I went to church every Sunday, even while we were on vacation. While I didn't always get a lot out of it, the discipline of attending a worship service every Sunday trained me to understand that my spiritual growth doesn't always come from emotional highs or lows. Sometimes it comes from just showing up. My family also had a great reverence for God. We were expected to dress up for church at a time when many didn't. It taught me to respect and revere God in a way we sometimes overlook today as we make God just our friend.

"I also had a great uncle who prayed constantly. He was old and sickly. His left leg had been amputated due to complications from diabetes, and he needed assistance just to get out of bed. He sat in a recliner in front of the television set every day, but he was blind, so he couldn't see it. His hearing was so bad he couldn't hear much either, but that man could pray! I remember seeing his lips move as he sat in his chair. All day he sat in a green chair and prayed. His circumstances were miserable, yet he was one of the most joy-filled people I ever knew. He was appreciative of the smallest things we did for him and thankful for everything. While

I don't have any specific recollections of his prayers, I always picture him sitting in the chair with his lips moving in prayer."

When Jennifer was in junior high school, her friend Karla was the first person to introduce her to the idea of a personal relationship with Jesus. "Until that time, I didn't understand that I could pray and talk to Him directly and that He could speak to me personally through the Bible. Understanding that I could have this kind of relationship with the Creator of the universe was a new concept for me and one that changed my life eternally."

Jennifer's friends and their families encouraged her spiritual growth through weekly Bible studies in their homes. After graduating from high school she lost touch with many of those friends, but each played an important part in developing her spiritual foundation.

## The Spiritual Legacy We Inherited

Each of us has inherited a faith influenced by others, a spiritual heritage, or possibly a lack of one. Maybe parents or grandparents played a key role in your faith, or perhaps it was friends or spiritual mentors at church, but chances are, if you have faith now, there was an adult who cared about your spiritual development when you were a child. Consider these statistics about adults who attended church as children:

- They are twice as likely to read the Bible as those who avoided church when they were young.[1]
- They are twice as likely to attend a church for worship on a typical weekend.[2]
- They are nearly 50 percent more likely to pray to God during a typical week.[3]

While not intentionally undertaken for this purpose, this research seems to confirm Prov. 22:6—"Train a child in the way he should go, and when he is old he will not turn from it."

It's easy to see how important spiritual inheritance and training is to the faith that we have today.

But what if the legacy we inherited isn't so good? Maybe we were taught that God is our Father, but our earthly father left us with a bad example of what a relationship with a father is all about. What if our parents never took us to church, or worse, like Snoozer, they turned us off from going to church once we could make our own decisions? Maybe the adults in our life used their religion as motivation for legalism or abuse, or maybe we feel devoid of a spiritual legacy—with nothing to pass on because there was nothing passed on to us.

If you find yourself in any of these circumstances, spend some time seriously examining your beliefs. You inherited a spiritual legacy—you just may not recognize it.

For example, maybe negative attitudes about churches or the clergy were passed on, or maybe it's the exact opposite—you learned to have an all-accepting attitude about church and God, believing it doesn't really matter because all roads lead to the same place in the end. If any of this sounds familiar, take time to study God's words as found in the Bible. Whether you inherited a faith-filled legacy, and especially if you didn't, there will come a point in your life when you can't live off your inheritance and you have to claim or reject the faith as your own. Now is that time. The best place to start is by reading the Bible and deciding whether the claims made there are true.

## Decreasing Inheritances

Unfortunately, as our culture has increasingly placed emphasis on other things, parents spend less and less time talking to their children about basic religious and moral issues such as truth, integrity, justice, and faith. As a result, the spiritual inheritance that each generation receives seems to be less than that of the last generation.

During a class on prayer in the adult Sunday School class we coteach for young married families, we discovered people who were eager to learn about praying aloud. They felt as if they weren't spiritual enough, or they weren't equipped to do it right, and they felt self-conscious when asked to pray in front of others. We observed that those who felt comfortable praying aloud started doing so when they were children, and those who felt anxious had not had an opportunity to pray aloud while they were young.

Could the fear of praying aloud be a result of families not having meals together? In previous generations, children learned to pray aloud at the dinner table where both kids and adults took turns saying the blessing before the meal. The children learned to model the behavior of their parents and had an opportunity to practice in a safe environment. Today, fewer families eat meals together because the dinner hour becomes a pit stop on the way to baseball or soccer practices. It's no wonder that we're creating a generation of people who aren't comfortable with praying out loud.

Further complicating this, many extended families no longer live near each other. When distance separates us physically, we're also spiritually separated from our heritage. Children are less likely to observe their grandparents' spiritual behavior when they see them only once or twice a year. Many of us have memories of a godly man or woman in our family who prayed with passion over holiday meals and who spoke openly about what God was doing in his or her life.

The recent anxiety about praying aloud could just be a symptom of a larger problem—the declining spiritual inheritance being passed on to subsequent generations.

## Passing on Spiritual Treasures

While we may have already received our spiritual inheritance, it's not too late to improve the spiritual legacy we leave. Paul writes to Timothy about the legacy that young man has inherited from his mother's side of the family: "I have been reminded of your sincere faith, which first lived in your grandmother Lois and in your mother Eunice and, I am persuaded, now lives in you also" (2 Tim. 1:5). Paul then tells Timothy that he can't live on that inheritance—he must build his spiritual life himself: "For this reason I remind you to fan into flame the gift of God, which is in you through the laying on of my hands" (v. 6).

Helen Kooiman Hosier has written a book based on many of the verses found in Timothy. It's titled *Living the Lois Legacy: Passing on a Lasting Faith to Your Grandchildren*. In the book she gives specific examples of grandparents who have made deliberate and conscious choices to pass their faith on to their grandchildren. Hosier encourages bonds between generations so the young can watch and observe from the past.

One of the best ways to do this is to encourage spiritual traditions during holiday celebrations. Even if we're celebrating with neighbors, friends, or coworkers, most people are more open to praying or discussing what they're thankful for before a holiday meal. For example, Joanne had to create new traditions for her family after her parents divorced. Thanksgiving became especially important, and she decided to purchase a special tablecloth that she puts out each year. With permanent marker, all guests write down something for which they're thankful and sign their names and date. Pulling out the tablecloth each year reminds her of what she has to be thankful for and the way God has worked in her life and the lives of her family and friends over the years. It's a tangible legacy in the form of an heirloom that her children will want to keep when she decides to pass it on.

It's important to share family members' spiritual successes, prayers that have been answered, miracles that have occurred, and how God has manifested His presence. To pass on an authentic faith, it's also important to share struggles, prayer burdens, unanswered prayers, and the questions we can't answer. Honesty about how we don't always understand but how we always choose to believe can do more to encourage others in their struggles than all the Pollyanna-ish answered prayers we can list. We can let others see our trials and tell them how God has brought us through, or even that we're waiting for God to bring us through. How we handle the obstacles in our lives and faith is more encouraging than any inspirational advice we can offer.

## Forcing a Legacy

When we think about leaving a spiritual legacy, we may be concerned about forcing our faith on others. Our current culture reinforces the belief that a separation of church and state should prohibit any discussion regarding faith, prayer, or God in any public environment. If we talk about our faith, we must be forcing it on someone who doesn't want to hear it, it's commonly believed.

The irony is that our nation was founded for people to have that freedom. One of the best spiritual legacies passed on to us by our forefathers is a respect and desire for people of faith to have freedom.

Maybe we've felt victimized by others who tried to force their ideas of religion on us. In some cases, people have been physically or emotionally harmed, even killed, in the name of religion. For most of us however, our suffering wasn't so dramatic. Perhaps we were required to memorize lengthy prayers, hymns, or Bible verses, and now we fear passing on the kind of negative memories that are a part of our spiritual legacy.

First, let's fix our past. Unless we were held at gunpoint or physically harmed during our spiritual tutoring, how we choose to view it is just that—a choice. As a child, if we viewed it as being forced to do things against our will, we might try to reconsider the circumstances now that we have some distance and perspective. Did those who required us to memorize verses do it to make money? Did our spiritual leaders get sadistic satisfaction at seeing us repeat rote words? Did they make us attend services because it made them look better? Or did the people who did those things do them out of love and a belief that they would help us? Maybe they did it as a response to Deut. 6:6-9:

> These commandments that I give you today are to be upon your hearts. Impress them on your children. Talk about them when you sit at home and when you walk along the road, when you lie down and when you get up. Tie them as symbols on your hands and bind them on your foreheads. Write them on the doorframes of your houses and on your gates.

Did they do it because they wanted to leave us a spiritual heritage? Understanding their motivation can help us to crystallize our own motivations in leaving a spiritual legacy to others.

Many people who spent time memorizing spiritual truths in their youth later came to see the benefits of that practice as God brought those truths to mind when they needed them most. Instead of it being a bad thing, or a forced thing, could it have been a good thing?

Imagine that those who required us to memorize scriptural truths knew that later in life we would struggle with depression so severe that we would contemplate suicide. Imagine they knew that when we were older we would be bedridden with cancer. Would we not expect them to do everything they could to prevent these things from happening? They would force us onto a strict diet, make us take medicines we didn't like, and maybe require us to undergo painful medical tests. Whether we liked it or not, they would force these things on us with the intention of saving us from the consequences of future disease.

Essentially, that's what spiritual training does. Teaching us how to pray or forcing us to memorize spiritual truths becomes an immunization for a disease many of us don't want to admit we have—sin. That spiritual preparation can help us avoid the effects of disease and deal more effectively with the consequences of it. Immunizations always involve the sting of the needle, but it's the price for immunity from a much greater and more painful disease.

The spiritual legacy we inherited was probably well-intentioned. Even Snoozer had good intentions, though the good that resulted in Craig's life wasn't exactly what Snoozer intended. The choice is ours. How we view our spiritual legacy and how we pass it on to the people we care about is the choice only we can make.

## A Conscious Spiritual Legacy

Maybe you feel inadequate about passing on a spiritual inheritance to your family. After all, who knows you and your faults better than your family? Maybe you already feel burdened by the consequences of your own weaknesses. Perhaps you find it hard to pray and read your Bible every day. Maybe you had premarital sex or experimented with drugs, and you think, *Who am I to tell others how to live as a Christian?*

If so, you may feel that you're not qualified to discuss spiritual things with others, especially with your children. Maybe you feel more comfortable leaving those kinds of conversation to the "experts" at church. But if you want your friends and family to inherit a spiritual legacy that will serve as a lifelong foundation for developing their faith, *you* have to make it a priority. Passing on faith isn't something that can be left to a pastor, a Sunday School teacher, or a passing missionary. You may be the only person who can speak to your brother or coworker. God uses us not to demonstrate what's right; He uses us to demonstrate our need for Him.

As for children, there are only a few years between when children are capable of understanding these concepts and when they will already have made up their minds. Recent research shows that nearly half of all Americans who accept Jesus Christ as Savior do so before reaching the age of 13, and that fewer than one out of four embrace Christ after turning 21.[4]

That means if we want our kids to have a spiritual legacy, we have only a few years, from the age of 5 or 6 to the age of 12, to help provide them with a foundation. While certainly many can and do make decisions outside that range, the research essentially points out the importance of parents deliberately passing on their spiritual values to children in that age-group. The people who will lead churches in 20 years are attending them now—they're in the preschool department, the children's classes, and the teen groups. What can we do to make sure they receive a rich spiritual heritage that will prepare them for their later roles?

What if we know someone outside those critical ages? Is it too late for him or her to develop a real faith? Absolutely not, but statistically speaking, it will likely be a friend, not an "expert" from church, who introduces that person to Jesus Christ. Are you that friend? Do you intentionally seek to pass on your spiritual legacy?

"In God we trust" can be a historical legacy, a slogan on a dollar bill, or how we live our lives. Our faith is a complicated fusion of what we were taught, whom we believed, and the faith traditions and history that went before us.

Ultimately, though, only you can take responsibility for your own faith and for the spiritual legacy you leave behind.

# 16
# Dysfunctional LEGACIES

Every family has a secret they don't like to talk about. Maybe it's a loony aunt. Maybe it's Grandpa's drinking. Maybe it's verbal or physical abuse. Maybe it's something worse.

Secrets like those become part of a negative legacy that we inherit from our families. How we choose to deal with them affects who we are. Sometimes problems come from the secret itself, and sometimes problems result from keeping the secret. Regardless of the secret we're trying to hide, the unspeakable legacies we inherit will affect the legacy we leave.

What's the secret in your family?

## Family Secrets

Anna grew up in a wealthy and politically connected family, with a beautiful mother and an adoring father—at least that's how it looked from the outside. Inside their home, Anna's mother publicly humiliated her, calling her ugly and discussing in front of others how homely she was. Anna's mother was the ultimate perfectionist; she was beautiful and socially graceful. Anna, however, was plain-looking. She had crooked teeth, a quivering high-pitched voice, and wore frumpy clothes—making her the perfect target for mocking by other children. No matter what she did, she could never live up to her mother's standards.

Anna's father loved his daughter despite her flaws. When he

was home he doted on her. He made great promises, most of which he couldn't keep. He was a heavy drinker, and his erratic behavior was consistent with that of an alcoholic. He disappeared for days on drinking binges. He became an embarrassment to his family, who eventually arranged to have him put into a mental asylum for treatment of his alcoholism.

While Anna's father was away and Anna was only eight, her mother died. She hoped she would be allowed to live with her father and take care of her two brothers. After his release, Anna did for a short time, but her father continued to drink. Her brother Elliott died within a year of their mother, and 18 months later, to Anna's great sadness, her father died also.

Anna and her little brother Hall, now orphans, went to live with their grandmother. But this new environment wasn't any better. The two drunken uncles who also lived there were considered so dangerous that locks had to be put on Anna's door. They would also take guns and shoot at the children from an upstairs window. Eventually this timid, sad little girl and her brother were sent to separate boarding schools, which further isolated her.

Hall did well in school and went on to Harvard, where he got his master's degree in engineering. He met his wife, and together they had three children. He had a good job, and all seemed well for a time, but eventually Hall wanted a divorce. He left his first wife and married again. That marriage lasted 12 years before it ended in divorce. Like his father, Hall's life was dominated by alcoholism. He died at the age of 50.

Difficult childhoods like Anna's and Hall's leave some people wounded and unable to contribute to society. For others, the difficulties they face as children become the motivation to change the world. That was the case for Anna Eleanor Roosevelt, better known as Eleanor Roosevelt, sister of Hall and wife of Franklin D. Roosevelt, the 32nd president of the United States.

Anna's experiences at the boarding school introduced her to new friends and a better way of relating. She grew intellectually, emotionally, and perhaps most important, socially. She married Franklin Roosevelt and blossomed as a woman and a political presence. She continued to develop her social skills throughout her life and discovered a passion for social work. Her devotion led to her participation in some of the greatest social changes our country had ever seen. The girl with the quivering voice eventually became the voice for those who didn't have one.

## Divorce for Generations

Joanne sat at the kitchen table talking to her husband. Though she was well into her 40s, she was still upset about having to be the one who negotiated where her family would spend Thanksgiving and Christmas each year. Her parents had divorced years ago, but family loyalties remained divided over whether her father, who had remarried twice, should be included in the celebrations.

Like stringing white lights from the trees and hanging wreaths with red bows, this conversation had become an annual holiday tradition for Joanne. But this year her teenage daughter sat at the table listening in as she tried to solve the unsolvable. "My brother isn't speaking to Dad, and Dad's new wife might not want to be around Mom." Her voice trailed off; there were no easy solutions. She looked up and saw the concern in her daughter's eyes; "See, Madison? That's what divorce does. Although the marriage ends, for the children the divorce never stops."

A divorce in the family means that the children must negotiate new traditions around a minefield of resentments, all the while trying to heal their own broken hearts. Jennifer doesn't remember the details of her grandparents' divorce, but she does remember the pain it caused her mother, Marie.

"Everyone knows that you want your parents to be there when you're little," said Marie, "but that feeling doesn't go away when you're older either." Marie recalls the bitterness that resulted from the initial break-up between her parents. "I remember that we kids couldn't talk to Dad. If we did, Mom thought we were betraying her—so when we spoke to him, we couldn't talk about it."

Marie knew she still wanted a relationship with her father despite the things he had done to cause the marriage to end. Trying to maintain that relationship while not upsetting her mother was a draining experience. In addition, she had to deal with her own grief over the breakup of her family.

## Consequences for Generations

In an earlier chapter we looked at the consequences of our behavior affecting our family up to the fourth generation. Nowhere is this more prevalent than in a family broken by divorce. While some marriages must end to stop the abuse in the family or because of sexual infidelity, in our culture divorce is often chosen because it seems easier to just start over. But it isn't. When divorce occurs, the probability that the couple's adult children will also divorce actually doubles.

Researchers offer several theories for this. Parents who divorce demonstrate a low commitment to marriage, and their children emulate that. Perhaps the "cause" of the divorce—disillusionment, poor communication, sexual infidelity, or lack of emotional control by one or both partners—is modeled for the children, who then imitate this behavior in their own marriages. Those problems are increased exponentially in a marriage in which both partners have divorced parents: their chance of divorce increases 189 percent.

Those behaviors are likely to continue for several generations, according to an article by Leslie Caste, who writes,

> The children of divorce are much more likely than the children of intact marriages to engage in the behaviors that increase the odds of divorce. Premarital cohabitation, lower educational attainment, marriage at early ages, lower socioeconomic achievement, and maternal employment all plague the children of divorce at higher rates than the children of intact marriages, and all contribute themselves to the likelihood of eventual divorce.[1]

Not that long ago, couples who had problems chose to stay together anyway, saying, "We're doing it for the children." They may not have known the data, but they still got it right. The consequences of divorce go on for generations when children are involved. Many people are familiar with the well-known poem "Children Learn What They Live." Divorce is a negative example of that poem. Divorce is an illustrative example of how our behavior and the resulting consequences affect future generations.

## Make Your Generation the Last

What if you're a product of divorce? How can you ensure that the negative legacy you've inherited isn't passed on to the next generation?

Divorce had an effect on Craig's family, but for him personally, it was actually a positive experience.

Craig's father, John, had one mother and two stepmothers as the result of his father's three marriages and two divorces. As expected, growing up in a divorced family caused emotional and physical hardships for him. John didn't even meet his father until he was 12 years old, and then he didn't have much contact with him until his sophomore year of college. John put himself through school and worked hard to get the education that many children of divorce aren't able to get because of the economic conditions that result when one household is split into two.

Fortunately for Craig and his brother, this personal history of failure simply meant that their dad was more determined than ever to have a successful marriage. John made many personal sacrifices for his family, yet he never complained and always let his wife and kids know that there was nothing more important to him than they were. Even John's second stepmother acknowledged that he had overcome his past to become a wonderful father and husband, making sure that his family would never experience the detrimental things he had.

How do we change the legacy we've inherited? It's simple—we change. We work especially hard to overcome the odds that are against us. We make deliberate choices to do things differently than our parents. We start living the legacy that we want our children to inherit by making the right choices, despite the wrong ones we may have grown up with.

## Overcoming Our Inheritance

While we may be eager to talk about the good, inspiring, or encouraging legacies we were left, most of us don't want to talk about the legacies that hurt us, humiliated us, and left invisible but very real scars. Yet those silent legacies are often the ones that have the biggest impact on future generations. If we've inherited or lived the consequences of a painful legacy, we know that it's like being wounded on a battlefield. The nearest hospital is too far away to be of any help, and those closest to us are too busy fighting their own battles. You have to stop your own emotional blood loss. But that's the question: How do you stop the loss of self, the loss of trust, the loss of love that results from those kinds of painful traumas?

For each person the process is different, but almost every case involves forgiveness. Saying those words sounds trite, but discovering the healing power of forgiveness and claiming that power for yourself can make you feel whole. Maybe the burdens you carry are not meant to be surmounted alone. Getting help from a professional counselor, minister, or trusted friend isn't a sign of weakness—it's recognizing that you want to stop the pain and that you don't want to pass it on to future generations.

To impart the kind of legacy you want to leave, sometimes you have to face the ugly legacy you inherited. In an earlier chapter we wrote about Nan, whose mother on her own deathbed called Nan stupid. Yet Nan chose to forgive. Craig's father, John, had a childhood scarred by divorce, yet he made deliberate choices to ensure that he would always be happily married to the same woman.

Eleanor Roosevelt has inspired generations. She could have lived a life like her brother's. Instead, she left a legacy of hope to those overcoming dysfunctional childhoods. She is an encouragement to those of us trying to do the same thing.

Many of us know someone who has overcome his or her past to leave a legacy different from the one he or she inherited. Perhaps you've even done it. But if your life is full of holes from the painful experiences you've lived, if you doubt yourself and your abilities, if you question whether you can ever find the wholeness you desire, you can look to the ultimate role model of overcoming obstacles—Jesus. No one is better at forgiving others' sins and overlooking the past.

# part 4

*But if you listen real close, you can hear them whisper
their legacy to you. Go on—lean in. Listen. You hear it?—Carpe—
hear it?—carpe, carpe diem; seize the day, boys.
Make your lives extraordinary.*
—Robin Williams as John Keating in the movie *Dead Poets Society* (1989)

*Not everyone is meant to make a difference. But for me,
the choice to lead an ordinary life is no longer an option.*
—Tobey Maguire as Peter Parker in the movie *Spider-Man* (2002)

*We are who we choose to be. . . . Now, CHOOSE!*
—Willem Dafoe as the Green Goblin in the movie *Spider-Man* (2002)

*My choice is you, GOD, first and only.
And now I find I'm your choice!*
—Ps. 16:5 (TM)

# 17
# A CHANGE
## for the
### Better

By this point we're beginning to feel as if our personal legacy could never be what we want it to be. There are things we must change to leave the kind of legacy we desire, and we realize that we'll have to make difficult choices to overcome some of our inherited legacies. Leaving the legacy we desire feels out of reach, and we may feel more like a part of the Jukes family than the Edwards. But even the best of legacies can come from an unimpressive lineage.

He was born in an obscure village, the child of a peasant woman. He grew up in another obscure village, where he worked in a carpenter shop until he was 30. Then, for three years, he was an itinerant preacher. He never had a family or owned a home. . . . He never traveled 200 miles from the place he was born. He never wrote a book or held an office. He did none of the things that usually accompany greatness.

While he was still a young man, the tide of popular opinion turned against him. His friends deserted him. He was turned over to his enemies and went through a mockery of a trial. He was nailed to a cross between two thieves. While he was dying, his executioners gambled for the only piece of property he had—his coat. When he was dead, he was taken down and laid in a borrowed grave.

Twenty centuries have come and gone, and today he is the central figure for much of the human race. All the armies that ever marched, and all the navies that ever sailed, and all the parliaments that ever sat, and all the kings that ever reigned, put together, have not affected the life of man upon this earth as powerfully as this one solitary life.

"One Solitary Life," adapted from a sermon made by James Allan Francis in 1926, beautifully illustrates the legacy of Jesus Christ. Jesus didn't inherit a perfect legacy despite the fact that He was the Son of God. Look at His genealogy as found in the first chapter of Matthew. Of the four women mentioned, all had questionable legacies. The first woman, Tamar, seduced her father-in-law to get pregnant. The second was Rahab, a prostitute. The third, Ruth, was disdained because she was a Moabite. The fourth, Bathsheba, was the woman with whom David committed adultery.

Let's not forget that Jesus was born to an unwed mother, one who claimed that she was pregnant through a divine conception. Her pregnancy was grounds for divorce, and she and Joseph weren't even married yet. Imagine the great familial and societal pressures Joseph had to overcome to stay with her. The whispering and mocking that went on behind his back must have been profuse. Imagine the self-doubt he must have had regarding that situation. Think of Jesus growing up in that kind of home with all that baggage to carry! The gossip probably subsided some when He was young, but as He got older and began to act strangely in the eyes of the locals, we can imagine that they discussed all the scandalous details once again.

Yet God knew that Jesus would be the perfect role model for us as we set out to create our own legacies. Jesus wasn't born into a perfect family. His parents made mistakes just as ours did. Yet as a man, Jesus was able to overcome all that. Despite His family, that one solitary life had greater impact in the world than any that went before or that will come after.

## Jukes and Edwards Revisited

Regardless of the legacy we may have inherited or created so far, change is still possible. Despite all the wonderful role models and examples of success in Jonathan Edwards's descendants, there were a few who didn't leave a legacy worthy of the family name. For example, his descendant Aaron Burr was a successful attorney who went on to become the vice-president of the United States. He had a successful law practice with Alexander Hamilton but always felt maligned by him. After years of contentious struggles, Burr chose to challenge Hamilton to a duel, and Hamilton felt he had no choice but to accept. That makes two bad choices. The duel went forward, and Burr killed his one-time friend and colleague.

Burr's legacy didn't get much better after that. He was later charged with treason but was eventually acquitted. He traveled to England but was thrown out of that country. Further travels left him penniless, so he couldn't afford a trip home for years. When he finally got back to the United States, he married his second wife. They separated four months later when she realized her fortune was dwindling away on his real-estate speculation. They finalized their divorce the day Burr died. Among such a well-respected family with such an impressive legacy, Burr was an anomaly that proves a legacy isn't just inherited—it's also chosen. Likewise, there are descendants of the Jukes family who pulled themselves out of poverty, were educated, and made something positive of their lives.

## A New Choice

It's all about the choices we make. For example, when we think of Richard Nixon, we think of his lying, and that's why we included him in a chapter on the importance of integrity. Though the scandal is decades old, it will forever be a part of his legacy. Many people who think of Nixon immediately think of Watergate. But this association isn't true for everyone who was involved in the scandal. It's not true of Chuck Colson.

If you've heard of Chuck Colson, it's likely that you associate the name with the organization he founded, Prison Fellowship Ministry, a non-profit group that works with churches to serve prisoners, ex-prisoners, crime victims, and their families. But you may not realize that he was also an integral part of the Watergate scandal.

As special counsel to President Richard Nixon, Colson was a true insider. Called Nixon's "hatchet man," Colson later admitted that he was guilty of doing whatever he had to in support of his president and his party, even stooping to "dirty tricks." According to the media at the time, Colson was "incapable of humanitarian thought." He pleaded guilty in 1974 to charges of obstruction of justice and spent seven months in jail.

Prior to going to jail, Colson was at a friend's house and heard him read aloud from C. S. Lewis's book *Mere Christianity*. The passage on pride spoke to Colson, who found himself sobbing in his car that night with a desire to know God. During the next week, he carefully studied *Mere Christianity* and accepted Jesus Christ as Lord of his life. Many were skeptical of his newfound faith.

In 1973, when a writer from the *Boston Globe* learned of his conversion, he wrote, "If Mr. Colson can repent of his sins, there just has to be hope for everybody." Colson was a man caught up in his own ego and political power, yet in coming to know Christ, he became a different person and will now leave an unbelievable legacy. He is an admirable person of faith, but he's also one of the greatest contemporary examples of someone who was able to change his legacy by changing the choices he made. More than 25 years later, skeptics are now believers. Colson's incredible worldwide ministry to prisoners and their families provides services to hundreds of thousands of people each year.

## True Convert

Perhaps the best historical example of someone changing his or her legacy is Saul, whom we know as Paul. We're familiar with him as one of the greatest evangelists who ever lived. He traveled widely, starting new churches and discipling believers. He trained many of the earliest Church leaders. He wrote 13 letters that are a part of the New Testament. But Paul wasn't always so zealous for Christ. In fact, as Saul, he zealously persecuted Christians.

Saul was dedicated to the law and his understanding of it as taught by the religious leaders of his day. He did everything he could to protect his beliefs—including persecuting the Christians he thought were heretics.

In an earlier chapter we called Adam a liar because he stood silently by when Eve and the serpent lied about God's words. Using that same reasoning, we would have to say that Saul was a killer. While the mob stoned the Christian evangelist Stephen for heretical beliefs in Jesus, Saul stood watch over their cloaks, fully supporting their actions.

While on the road to Damascus, Saul had a life-changing experience. Blinded by a great light, he fell to the ground and heard a voice ask, "Saul, Saul, why do you persecute me?" When Saul asked who the voice was, the response was "I am Jesus, whom you are persecuting" (Acts 26:14-15).

Blind Saul was taken to Damascus to the house of believers, who cared for him for three days. On the third day, the Lord asked a fellow believer, Ananias, to go minister to Paul. While many may have been skeptical of Colson's conversion, those who knew Saul were terrified of his. What if he was just pretending so he could get closer to the Christians he was hunting? Ananias argued with God until he was convinced this is what God wanted. He went where Saul was staying and laid his hands on Saul's eyes. Immediately the scales fell away, Saul was no longer blind, and he was baptized right then.

Saul wasted no time in telling people about his conversion. In fact, his preaching so worked up the crowds in Damascus that they were waiting for him near every exit to the city to kill him. The only way for him to leave was in a basket thrown over the wall.

The Lord had warned Ananias that Saul would suffer in Christ's name, and he did. After his conversion, Saul was better known by his Hebrew name, Paul. He endured beatings with whips and rods, a stoning, three shipwrecks, imprisonment, hunger, thirst, cold, and nakedness. Yet as we pointed out in chapter 14, Paul was the one who later urged us to rejoice in our sufferings.

Is there a more incredible example of a legacy change? A man who was against everything about Jesus eventually became the greatest Jesus promoter and follower who ever lived. Not only did his legacy change on a public level from a man who hated Jesus to a man who loved Jesus, but Paul had changed as a man as well. As Saul, he loved the law more than anything else. His physical presence was intimidating to all Christians. But as Paul, intimidation was replaced with intimacy, as he taught and mentored many early believers. As evidenced by the letters he wrote to his friends, Paul became a kind and tenderhearted man who loved people.

Regardless of what legacy we have created or inherited, it's possible to change that legacy for a better one. Jesus was born to a lineage of sinners, yet His is the one solitary life that has most powerfully affected so many lives on this earth. Chuck Colson changed from a hatchet man into the leader of a prison ministry, positively affecting some of the most disenfranchised and forgotten people in our society. Saul changed from a Christian persecutor into the most persuasive evangelist who ever lived.

## Create the Legacy You Desire

How do we explain the dramatic changes that took place in the legacies of Colson and Saul? Both of them changed their legacy so dramatically that the deeds done in the second half of their lives dramatically overshadowed those done in the first half. What can we learn from them to create the legacy we desire?

Both of them had a personal encounter with Jesus that made them understand the sin in their lives. Saul, knocked to the ground, heard Jesus personally accuse him of persecution.

In an interview with *Jubilee* magazine, Colson described his moment this way,

> Until that moment in that driveway, I had always thought that God was like any college professor who grades on a curve. I wasn't much worse than anyone else. That night I was a guy trapped—overwhelmed by the stench of my own sin. Not the stuff that was in Watergate. That was child's play. But I thought about myself, the people I had hurt, my insensitivities, my self-centeredness, my pride.[1]

While neither man looked into the eyes of Jesus in a literal sense, both stood face-to-face with Him, and each had to decide how he would respond. In the same interview, Colson discussed that C. S. Lewis's book *Mere Christianity* helped him make sense of that encounter: "Lewis forced me to understand the choice I had to make. He made what happened in Tom's driveway reasonable, logical, and rational."[2]

Saul spent three days in Damascus trying to make sense of the choice presented to him. Both chose to follow Jesus. But it wasn't a choice made with just words, because both immediately put into action the choice they made.

In both cases, outsiders had trouble believing that the conversion was real. The Christians were fearful of Saul, and the media was skeptical of Colson. Yet neither man wavered in his decision and set about doing what he felt the Lord called him to do. At times, they had to explain their backgrounds or justify their decisions to those who questioned them. For both, it wasn't their words that convinced observers—it was their actions.

Both men suffered for what they believed, both had their lives threatened, and both served time in prison and used that time to further their legacies. Each man had a plan and a mission, but each formed a partnership with local churches to work out the plan. Their personal legacies proved to be consistent with their public legacies.

While both of them have books, Paul's has sold more copies. Neither grew financially rich. However, both have rich legacies that will last for generations of their own friends and families— but also for more distant observers whose lives are changed from watching these men of faith and action and seeing Christ in them.

Throughout this book, we've encouraged you to take action on your own legacy. We've talked about the importance of being deliberate and thoughtful in your choices. What we do affects the people around us now and later. If you act with integrity, establish a balance with your time and family, and spend your money with the knowledge that it isn't really yours, you take steps to create a positive legacy. Replacing bad habits with disciplined practices, honoring your marital vows in every way, and making sure your actions speak as loudly as your words are just a few of the ideas we've discussed.

Essentially, these things add up to identifying your priorities and choosing to align your behavior with those priorities. And like Colson and Paul, we believe that your first priority should be Jesus. If you look around and see dramatically changed lives, you'll usually find that they center on Jesus. No other person has so influenced the lives and legacies of so many.

## What Jesus Says Is Most Important

The religious leaders of Jesus' day were confronted with long lists of dos and don'ts, and one day they came to Him asking which one was the most important. Perhaps you have the same question when you look at all the things we've talked about. What's the most important thing you can do to leave a positive legacy?

Jesus' answer to those leaders is also the most important advice we can offer: "Love God with all your heart, soul, mind, and strength, and love your neighbor as yourself."

Putting God first in your life makes everything else fall into place. If you understand that you're merely God's creation— though a very special and very loved creation—you won't make the mistake of thinking you're the one who should be in control. You'll base your decisions on something far greater than your own self-interest.

To love your neighbors as yourself doesn't mean to deny self— rather, it implies that you must first love and respect yourself so that you can love and respect others. Jesus is telling you that He values you. Likewise, you need to value yourself. Being healthy means taking care of your body, but loving yourself and others means taking care of your own emotional needs. It's only when you're healthy physically and mentally that you can serve others. You won't get in trouble from having a healthy self-esteem but rather by trying to justify why you're more important than others.

If you consider the things that make up a positive legacy, all of them are summed up in that one command "Love God with all your heart, soul, mind, and strength, and love your neighbor as yourself." Following this command will help you achieve the kind of legacy you desire to leave.

# 18
# Love for
# a THOUSAND
# Generations

In the last chapter we said that the greatest thing we can do for our legacies is to keep what Jesus called the greatest commandment: "Love God with all your heart, soul, mind, and strength, and love your neighbor as yourself." Why is that the greatest commandment? Because more than anything else, that's what God does. He loves all of us unconditionally. He loves us and our weird neighbors. It's like a great present. We don't have to earn it, and we don't have to work at it—we just have to show up, and He loves us.

There are countless examples of people who followed that advice and subsequently left great legacies. Perhaps the most interesting one is the legacy of King David. David was a man who truly loved God. In fact, the Bible calls him "a man after [God's] own heart" (Acts 13:22).

David wrote 73 psalms of praise and worship to God. Each one articulated that sensitive man's emotion. At the same time, he was very much a man's man. When David was just a teenager, Goliath, a Philistine man who stood nine feet tall, threatened King Saul and his armies, but no one dared to stand up to him. David, however, had the right perspective. Angered by the fact that Goliath was insulting his God, he took his slingshot, and in an act of incredible bravery, he killed the giant. While it may have been considered a brave act by others, for David it was an act of faith and love.

That encounter was the beginning of David's distinguished career. During his life he had many military, political, and spiritual accomplishments. The dynasty he founded ruled the nation from 1010 B.C. until its fall to the Babylonians in 586 B.C.

But like many who've had great success at work, David's home life was disappointing. In a previous chapter, we talked about David and Bathsheba. That wasn't David's only fall into temptation, but it was one of his greatest. It was a classic example of sexual abuse, with David as the powerful abuser and Bathsheba the victim. In many cases of abuse, the secret shame of the victim can never be overcome. The abuser may apologize and make repeated promises to change, but the cycle continues, sometimes into the next generation. David later offered us an example of true contrition.

Confronted with his sins by Nathan the prophet, David wrote Psalm 51, in which he publicly exonerated Bathsheba and took full responsibility for his actions. In it, he publicly begged God for grace and mercy and, most of all, forgiveness, which God granted. His actions ultimately laid a foundation for a loving relationship with Bathsheba. She later bore him four sons, one of whom was Solomon, who inherited David's throne. While there was great hope in David's ability to be restored to his wife and to his God, the consequences of his choices lingered.

In *Every Man of the Bible*, Larry Richards writes about David as a father:

> David was at best a passive parent. David cared deeply but was never willing to step forward. David neither disciplined nor counseled. He neither confronted nor forgave. David's inaction seems to have been perceived by David's children as indifference; an indifference that left them free to cross the boundary between right and wrong.[1]

Richards continues, asking the reader why David detached himself from his family, and answers his own question:

> Some assume it was the press of great affairs—for David had a kingdom to manage. But I suspect that the underlying reason was David's earlier failure with Bathsheba, which, despite God's forgiveness and her forgiveness, too, robbed him of that moral authority that every parent needs. Seeing his own

flaws repeated in his children, David seems to have drawn back, feeling helpless.[2]

Richards is saying that despite his behavior, David could still choose what kind of parent he would be. This is exactly the point of this book. Regardless of what has happened in your past or your family's lineage, the choice remains with you.

Part of David's punishment for his transgressions was that God did not allow him to build the Temple that he passionately desired to build. Instead, God allowed his son to do it. Solomon built the Temple in Jerusalem and fulfilled his father's dream. He ruled for 40 years and was known for the great wisdom God granted him. He made brilliant business decisions, including signing peace treaties with the surrounding nations, which increased his personal prosperity and brought peace for his nation. As was the custom, he sealed many of those treaties by marrying into the various royal families.

Despite the prohibitions in the law against marrying foreigners, Solomon eventually had 700 wives. His foreign-born wives worshiped idols, which he allowed them to do, and even built shrines to enable their worship. Eventually the wives persuaded him to join them in their false worship, and he did, resulting in his personal fall.

We might assume that Solomon died a rich and happy man. Instead, he concluded in his Book of Ecclesiastes that all of life's accomplishments are meaningless apart from God. Solomon had everything—earthly riches beyond compare. Think of the Forbes list of billionaires all combined under only one name—Solomon. But at the end of his life, separated from God, Solomon felt that life was meaningless.

Did David's legacy of poor choices affect Solomon and his other children? Did Solomon learn how to make bad choices from David, or did he inherit the consequences of his father's poor choices? Or both? While it's hard to know which is the cause and which is the effect, obviously the actions of the preceding generation affected the next generation.

In chapter 5 we talked about Exod. 20:5, which said that God would "[punish] the children for the sins of the fathers to the third and fourth generation of those who hate [him]." Essentially, we pointed out that we show hatred toward God through our actions of disobedience. While David and Solomon were both men who loved God, there were obvious cases of disobedience in both their lives. Ultimately, which one counts more? The actions that demonstrated their love or the disobedience that showed hate?

Disobeying God means that the consequences of our sins will be passed on to the third or fourth generation. But the Bible also has great promises for those who love God. The verse that follows our theme verse says, "showing love to a thousand generations of those who love me and keep my commandments" (Exod. 20:6).

Think about this. The bad stuff we do has consequences, and those consequences may affect our families for three or four generations. But loving and obeying the Lord has rewards that go on for a thousand generations. Thus, the rewards for loving God are infinitely better than the consequences of disobeying Him. Regardless of what we may have been brought up to believe about a harsh or judgmental God, He is incredibly forgiving and loving, especially when, like David, we truly seek His forgiveness. As we saw with David, it doesn't make the consequence of our poor choices disappear, but it does ensure that the rewards for loving Him continue.

Is there any proof of this?

Go back to Jesus' genealogy. Despite the sins of David and Solomon, Jesus was actually born of their lineage. Ruth was a part of that genealogy. Moabites were not allowed into the Temple of the Lord to the tenth generation because of their lack of concern for the Israelites. Ruth's choice to leave the land of the Moabites with Naomi, her mother-in-law, and return to the land of the Israelites dramatically changed her inherited Moabite legacy. She went from not being allowed in God's Temple to being in the direct lineage of God's Son.

Imagine what God has planned for us if we're deliberate about our choices.

The legacy we leave is the sum of the seemingly insignificant decisions we make. Our legacies will live on in those who casually observed us from afar, in those who knew us best, and most important, in God's eyes, long after we're gone. When we think about how we want to be remembered, we must think long-term. We determine our own legacies, whether it's to the fourth generation or to the thousandth.

If your choice includes loving God, your legacy on earth will be unforgettable—lasting for a thousand generations—and your reward will be eternal.

# Notes

## Chapter 1
1. No relation to the coauthor.

## Chapter 2
1. Sources differed slightly on some of the details used in this chapter. We relied heavily on the following two sources, though when possible details were checked against others:

Estabrook, Arthur H. (June 17, 2004), "The Jukes in 1915," Carnegie Institution of Washington, <http://www.disabilitymuseum.org/lib/docs/759.htm#6>.

Winship, A. E. *Jukes-Edwards: A Study in Education and Heredity.* Harrisburg, Pa.: R. L. Meyers & Co., 1900.

## Chapter 4
1. Details were taken from news and television reports and from Tom Barbash, *At the Top of the World* (New York: Harper Collins Publishers, 2002).

## Chapter 5
1. Ps. 45:7; Amos 5:15; Matt. 6:24; Luke 16:13.
2. J. G. McConville, *Apollos Old Testament Commentary, Deuteronomy* (Downers Grove, Ill.: Intervarsity Press, 2002), 127.

## Chapter 7
1. Leesa Bellesi, interview by Jennifer Schuchmann, October 6, 2004.

## Chapter 9
1. "Child-proofing on the World Wide Web: A Survey of Adult Web-servers," 2001, Jurimetrics. National Research Council Report, 2002.
2. UK News Telegraph, NOP Research Group, January 7, 2002.
3. Maryann B. Hunsberger (September 18, 2004), "The Road Home," <http://www.christianitytoday.com/music/interviews/2004/sandipatty-0904.html>.
4. "Born-Again Christians Just as Likely to Divorce as Are Non-Christians," The Barna Group, September 8, 2004. <www.barna.org>

## Chapter 10
1. Mike Klingman (September 22, 2004), "Out of game, out of sorts for O's budding 'Iron Man'" <http://www.baltimoresun.com/sports/baseball>.

2. Thomas Boswell (September 22, 2004), "Ripken's Two Grand: No Mean Streak," <http://www.washingtonpost.com/wp-srv/sports/longterm /memories/cal/rip94bos.htm>.

**Chapter 11**

1. Jerry MacGregor, "Mentoring," in *Stories for the Heart*, ed. Alice Gray (Sisters, Oreg.: Multnomah Press, 1996), 101-102.

**Chapter 15**

1. "Adults Who Attend Church as Children Show Lifelong Effects," The Barna Group, November 5, 2001. <www.barna.org>

2. Ibid.

3. Ibid.

4. "Evangelism Is Most Effective Among Kids," The Barna Group, October 11, 2004. <www.barna.org>

**Chapter 16**

1. Leslie Carbone (November 5, 2004), "The Divorce Caste," <http: //www.pfm.org/AM/Template.cfm?Section=BreakPoint1&template=/CM /HTMLDisplay.cfm&ContentID=6109>.

**Chapter 17**

1. <http://www.pfm.org/Am/Template.cfm?Section=PFM_Site&tem plate=/cm/HTML/Display.cfm?ContentID=2108>

2. Ibid.

**Chapter 18**

1. Larry Richards, *Every Man of the Bible* (Nashville: Thomas Nelson Publishers, 1999), 57.

2. Ibid.